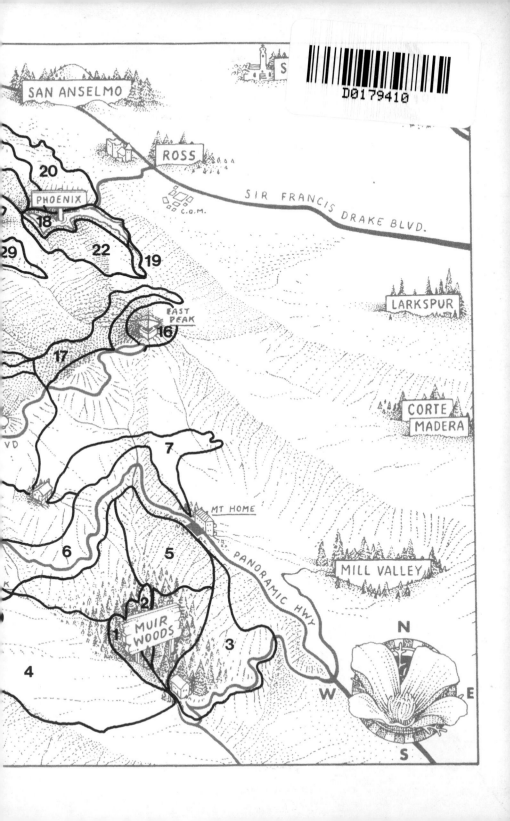

SAN ANSELMO

ROSS

SIR FRANCIS DRAKE BLVD.

20

PHOENIX

18

29

22

19

C.G.M.

LARKSPUR

EAST
PEAK

16

17

CORTE
MADERA

7

MT HOME

6

5

PANORAMIC HWY

MILL VALLEY

2

MUIR
WOODS

1

3

4

N

W   E

S

MT TAM

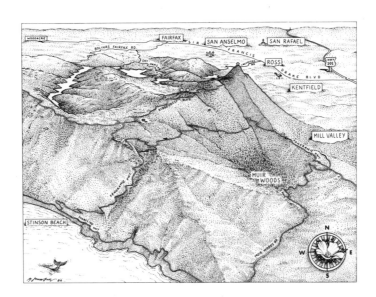

A Hiking, Running and Nature Guide

Don and Kay Martin

illustrated by Bob Johnson

Acknowledgements

The roots of Indian paintbrush, genus *Castilleja*, spread out underground and physically attach themselves to the roots of nearby plants. So when we see the bright red or orange blossom of the paintbrush in spring, we know it does not act alone. It draws moisture, nutrients and support from plants around it.

The book is like the paintbrush. It has received the nourishment, encouragement and advice of many friends and experts. For sharing their resources, we would like to thank

Marilyn Englander, Lincoln Fairley, Wilma Follette, Jim Furman, Dave Gould, Mary Johnson, Jim Locke, Greg Martin, Susan Martin, Casey May, Eric McGuire, Candace McKinnon, Jerry Olmsted,Ken Perez, Stephen Petterle,Tom Parker, Fred Sandrock, Bob Stewart, Meryl Sundove, Mia Monroe Way and the

California Native Plant Society
Marin Community College Biology Department
Marin Municipal Water District
Marin Museum of the American Indian
Mt Tamalpais History Project
Mt Tamalpais State Park
Muir Woods National Monument
San Francisco State University Botany Department
and the public libraries and librarians of Marin County.

Although these people and organizations have provided valuable support, we are responsible for all errors that have occurred.

TABLE OF CONTENTS

How To Use This Guide

This section offers a few suggestions on how to use this book.

Who Should Use This Guide
*Casual hikers wanting to enjoy the great outdoors.
*Runners searching for new running trails.
*Nature lovers pursuing varied flora and birds.
*Wildflower fans seeking the annual spring color parade.
*Experienced hikers exploring new trails.
*Visitors looking for the Bay Area's greatest views.

In short, this book is for anyone who wants to experience the beauty, grandeur and quiet majesty of the wildflowers, creeks, waterfalls, redwoods, chaparral and views offered by Mt Tamalpais.

Choosing A Hike Or Run
The easiest way to choose a hike or run is to select one from the map shown on the inside cover. Another way to use this book is to thumb through the hikes to find one that sounds good, then take off. The two most important factors to consider when choosing a hike or a run are distance and elevation change. These two factors, plus the footing conditions and the trail's steepness, determine the hike's overall difficulty.

Distance and elevation information are given in the introduction to each hike. The running rating (see below) provides footing information while the hike description can be skimmed to check on the trails steepness. If you are new to the mountain or new to hiking or running, it's best to choose a hike or run conservatively. Three miles of hiking or running on the mountain can take twice as long and can be twice as hard as three miles on flat terrain.

Once you've selected a range of distances and elevations, there are several questions you might consider. What is the best hike for this season? What wildflowers are in bloom now? Are they on this hike? Where are the best view hikes? The best hikes in hot weather? A good place to begin answering these questions is to look at the suggested hikes in Appendix A2, A3 and A4. Parking also can be a factor in choosing a hike. The section, Getting There, tells how to get to the starting points and describes parking conditions.

The Hiking Rating
If you're wondering how we arrived at the various ratings used in this

book, here is a brief description of the method used.

The hiking rating depends on aesthestics. How interesting is the hike? For example, the Simmons - Cataract Trails, Hike 13, has great flora, terrain and trails and often follows a creek. We consider it interesting 95-100% of the time and so, rated it a 10. On the other hand, the Taylor Trail - Bullfrog Rd, Hike 25, goes mostly along roads and, in some areas, has little change in flora. We consider it interesting about 55-60% of the time and rated it a 6.

Obviously, this rating system is subjective and depends on what we like. Also, the rating system is dependent on the season. For example, the Coastal Trail, Hike 12, is magnificent in the spring when the hills are green and the flowers bloom. It is rated a 10. However, in summer, the hills are dry and tall thistles crowd the trail, so even though the views are still great, the hike is no longer a 10. The rating of hikes is based on the best conditions, the best season, views, weather and wildflowers.

Running Rating

The running rating is based solely on footing conditions. We consider stairs, rocky paths, exposed roots and steep slopes to be poor footing conditions. If a trail has poor footing 0-5% of the time, it is rated a 10. Each additional 5% of poor footing reduces the running rating by 1 point. For example, the North Side Trail, Hike 17, is quite rocky or steep about 40-45% of the time so the running rating is reduced eight points to leave a running rating of 2.

Distance Measurements

The distance measurements were determined by a combination of five methods.

*Distances were taken from trail signs.

*Odometer readings from a mountain bike were taken on roads.

*Distances were measured on various maps with a map meter.

*Mileage was taken from the Tamalpais Conservation Club map.

*Hikes and runs were timed and converted to distance.

Distances between mileage points are probably accurate to 0.1 miles, while overall distances are good to 0.2 miles.

Elevation Change

The elevation change was taken from USGS maps. For hikes that make one long trip up, then down, the elevation change is fairly accurate. A few trails like the Pumpkin Ridge and High Marsh Trails behave like a rollercoaster and elevation information is less accurate.

When To Go Rating

The when to go rating is based on flora, weather, season, views, trail and road conditions. Because Mt Tamalpais has a Mediterranean climate, winters provide rainfall and water runoff, while late winter and spring provide wildflowers and these are the best times to go on most hikes.

Disclaimer

Trails change, roads change, weather changes, plants change, trees fall down, signs change and hikes change. In winter, some trails and roads may be impassable. This book is only a guide. We can not accept responsibility for trail conditions or for trail information. Although we have tried to provide the best information possible, there may be typographical and content mistakes. This is our disclaimer that we do not accept liability or legal responsibility for any injuries, damage, loss of direction or time allegedly associated with using this book. To be certain of the best information available, you should always check at the local Ranger Station before starting a hike or run.

Precautions

Poison oak for some is a minor irritation, for most, a major irritation

 and for a few, a medical emergency. The best advice is to learn to identify the plant by its leaves and avoid touching it. An old saying is, "Leaves of three, leave it be." In fall, poison oak leaves turn crimson red and drop off. In winter, the bare branches are difficult to identify, yet still retain their toxic oils. It helps to stay on designated trails and to watch out for branches that lean out onto the trail or drape down over the path. Poison oak is very common on the mountain.

Fire is a part of the natural history of the mountain. However, in recent years, fire control has left some parts of the mountain with excessive deadwood and inflammable material. At times, the mountain constitutes an extremely dangerous fire hazard and access to parts of it is closed. Park and Water District authorities are trying to remedy the situation with controlled burns in off-season times. In all cases, fires are permitted only in permanent barbecues and in Muir Woods, smoking is prohibited.

Fluids are essential when hiking or running. Often, people go hiking or go to the beach and wind up the day with a mild headache. Usually, this is attributed to too much exposure; too much sun or too much

3

wind. Many times, the problem is too little fluids. Hiking or running requires a minimum of 1/2 quart of fluids per hour and often more, depending on the temperature and elevation change. It is always a good idea to carry water on a hike and to drink it whether you feel thirsty or not.

Litter is not a big problem on Mt Tamalpais. Compared to other areas, the mountain is quite clean. There are probably two reasons for this. First, most people and most groups who use the mountain treat it with great respect. Second, many people have been influenced by one of Marin's foremost naturalists. Before Mrs Terwilliger begins a hike, she takes a trash bag around and picks up litter in the area. Her example and activities have inspired thousands of children, and adults too, to care for mother earth with enthusiasm and courtesy.

Using The Maps

The top map on each page has been drawn to provide an aerial overview of the hike's location, view areas and general terrain. Roads, lakes, major peaks and major ridges are shown, but the map was not drawn to show details. Details are provided on the individual hike maps that show trail and road locations using the following symbols.

Trail used for hike or run	▬▬▬▬	Nearby Trail	―――――
Road used for hike or run	████████	Nearby dirt road	⬛⬛⬛⬛
Nearby paved road	⬛⬛⬛⬛		

Identifying Flora

Each hike description includes information on wildflowers and plant communities that may be found on the hike. Appendices A12 to A14 describe the plant communities in more detail and include a sketch of the leaves of the most common plants. Wildflowers are described in detail in Appendices A8 to A11. Wildflowers are identified in hikes using their common names. Sometimes, we use one common name to refer to more than one species of a flowering plant. For example, there are three species of lupine on the mountain, but we do not distinguish between them in the hike description. In the Appendix, we describe just one species of each kind of wildflower.

No matter how you use this book, we hope that you will enjoy the mountain as much as we have in preparing this guide. Hiker or runner, first-time casual visitor or old-timer, this book will help you discover the secrets and joys of Mt Tamalpais.

Getting There

Getting to the North Side Starting Points
Take Highway 101 to Sir Francis Drake Blvd (SFD) and follow SFD through Kentfield to Ross.

Natalie Greene Park in Ross
From SFD: Take Lagunitas Rd left to the end of the road. Parking is limited, often full. Parking is okay in the street, but beware of No Parking areas.
Nearest bus: #20 stops every half hour at SFD and Lagunitas Rd.

Continuing to the North Side Starting Points
Continue on SFD to San Anselmo and go left at the "hub", a junction just past the San Anselmo theater. Stay on SFD to Fairfax, turn left on Pacheco, then right on Broadway, to pass in front of the Fairfax theater. Just past the Fairfax theater, turn left on Bolinas Avenue.

Deer Park in Fairfax
From Bolinas Ave: Turn left on Porteous Ave and follow it as it winds around to Deer Park. Parking is limited.
Nearest bus: Every half hour, #23 eastbound on SFD, westbound on Broadway, both stops near Bolinas Ave.

South Side Starting Points
From Highway 101, take the Shoreline Hwy (Hwy 1) turnoff, signed to Mt Tamalpais and Stinson Beach. Follow the Hwy 1 signs for three windy miles, then turn right on Panoramic Hwy.

Muir Woods
From Panoramic Hwy: After about one mile, take the poorly marked and dangerous Muir Woods turnoff to the left. At Muir Woods, parking is limited. Rangers prefer that hikers (in contrast to visitors) park in the lower annex parking lot farthest from the entrance.
Nearest bus: #63 at Mt Home or Pantoll on weekends only.

Mt Home - Bootjack - Pantoll
From Panoramic Hwy: The Panoramic Hwy passes each of these areas in turn. Parking is limited, but best at Bootjack.
Nearest bus: #63 stops at each location about four times a day on weekends only. Check the Golden Gate Transit schedules.

Bon Tempe Dam outside Fairfax
From Bolinas Ave: Turn left on Sky Oaks Rd and go up to the toll booth (pay fee). About 1/2 mile past the toll booth, turn right on the dirt road. Limited parking at the dam, but more parking by Alpine Lake. Nearest bus: #23 in Fairfax.

Lagunitas Lake outside Fairfax
From Bolinas Ave: Same as Bon Tempe directions, only stay on the paved road from the toll booth to the end. Lots of parking here. Nearest bus: #23 in Fairfax.

Alpine Lake Dam outside Fairfax
From Bolinas Ave: Stay on Bolinas Ave to the dam. Limited parking. Nearest bus: #23 in Fairfax.

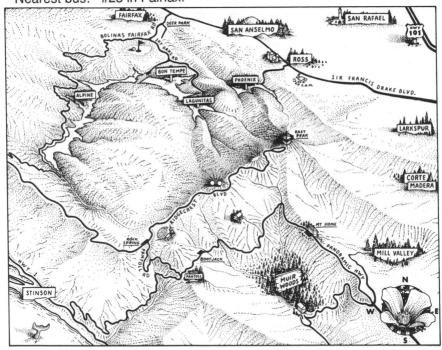

Rock Spring
From Panoramic Hwy: Stay on Panoramic Hwy to Pantoll, then go right on Pantoll Rd. Rock Spring is at the next junction. Nearest Bus: #63 at Pantoll.

East Peak
From Rock Spring: Head right on Ridgecrest Blvd. Good parking.

6

1 Muir Woods - Hillside Trail

Distance: 1.9 miles
Elevation Change: 200'
Rating: Hiking - 10   Running - No, too crowded.
When to Go: Excellent anytime, best in February and March.
This Muir Woods hike is the most heavily traveled trail on Mt Tam as it winds along the floor of a beautiful virgin redwood forest.

0.0 Start at the Muir Woods parking lot. Follow the signed Main Trail along the right side of Redwood Creek. The trail has several nature information signs describing the redwood forest. Look for white milkmaids and pink trillium in late winter.
0.5 Cathedral Grove. A beautiful redwood grove dedicated to the founding of the United Nations in San Francisco in 1945. Tanoak and western swordfern are the dominant shrub-like growth under the redwood canopy, while redwood sorrel provides most of the ground cover. Ahead, the light green leaves of western azalea, hazel and big leaf maple stand out under the dark green redwood background.
0.7 Junction with Fern Creek. Continue left. Notice how some redwoods have an enormous number of sprouts growing out of the base, while others have a grey-green lichen growth on the bark.
0.9 Park boundary and junction. Bear left, cross the bridge and head up to Hillside Jct. Go left again for a gentle climb.
1.1 Ravine. The first of three small picturesque ravines. Ferns, mosses, pink trillium, sorrel and the striking clintonia lie along the bank. Notice the large Douglas fir just past the streambed. Its bark differs from nearby redwoods in texture and in the moss covering. Redwoods often have lichens, but seldom moss.
1.2 Quiet redwoods. Several times, the trail passes very close to large redwoods and you can hear the difference.
1.6 Junction. The Hillside Trail gently descends to the canyon floor. Stay right to enter Bohemian Grove with some of the tallest trees in the park, nearly 260'. Ahead at the bridge, look for spawning silver salmon and steelhead trout in wintertime.
1.8 Snack shop, gift shop and restroom facilities.
1.9 Parking lot. Continue walking along the creek to see several large red alders in a riparian setting. Further on down, across from the highway entrance, notice the incredibly tangled buckeye trees with moss-covered trunks criss-crossing every which way.

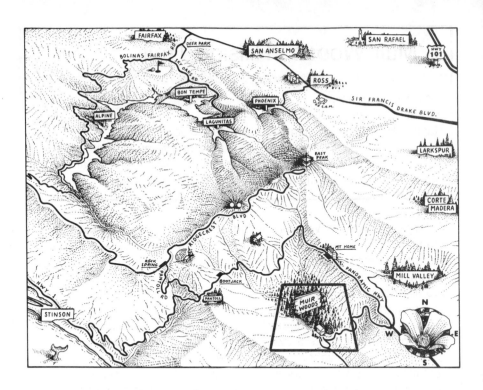

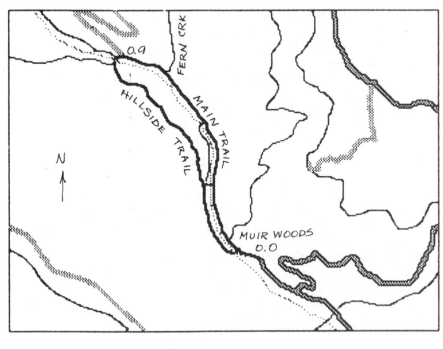

2 Muir Woods - Fern Creek

Distance: 3.6 miles
Elevation Change: 300'
Rating: Hiking - 9   Running - 9
When to Go: Excellent anytime, best in February and March.
This is a great redwood forest hike that leaves the crowded Muir Woods floor to explore around Fern Creek and Camp Alice Eastwood.

0.0 Start at the Muir Woods parking lot. Follow the signed Main Trail along the right side of Redwood Creek. The trail has several nature information signs describing the redwood forest. Look for white milkmaids and pink trillium in late winter.
0.7 Junction with Fern Creek. Head right along the small creek. Watch for the striking pink clintonia flower in April.
0.9 Bridge. The first of three bridges over Fern Creek. Watch for clusters of ladybugs along the creek from May to October.
1.1 Junction and bridge. Bear left down the 50 foot bridge. Continue upstream on the left bank to another junction. Then, either take the shortcut up the stairs, or go slightly further upstream. Look for iris as the trail climbs through the redwoods.
1.8 Plevin-Cut and Camp Alice Eastwood junctions. At the first junction, continue right. The camp, named for Alice Eastwood, avid botanist, writer and hiker, was dedicated in 1949 on her 90th birthday. From the camp, cross the paved parking circle to the road signed to Muir Woods. The road starts down and briefly enters an open area of broom, madrone, manzanita, oak and yerba santa.
2.5 Junction. Take the signed Bootjack Spur trail right past a large lichen-covered redwood tree down to Redwood Creek, then go left and head downstream. Look for spawning salmon and steelhead trout in late winter. Notice the light green leaves of western azalea, hazel and big leaf maple against the dark green background.
2.7 Junction and Park boundary. Continue along the left side of the creek with tanoak and huckleberry along the path.
3.1 Bridge and Cathedral Grove. Cross the bridge to return down the right side of Redwood Creek. Look for redwood burls. Further ahead is Bohemian Grove with some of the tallest trees in the park at 260'. Just past the grove, two red alders have a heavy coat of moss on their trunks. Nature signs describe the undergrowth.
3.6 Snack shop, gift shop, restroom facilities and parking lot.

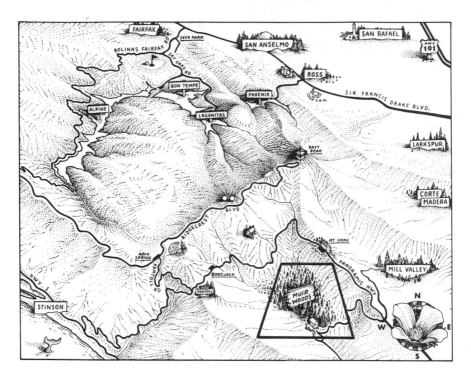

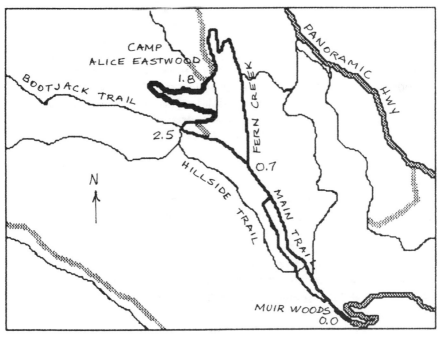

3 Panoramic - Sun Trails

Distance: 4.2 miles
Elevation Change: 700'
Rating: Hiking - 9   Running - 5
When to Go: Good anytime, best February to April.
A great hike out of Muir Woods into mixed conifers, then on to the
Sun Trail where wildflowers start in early February.

0.0 At the Muir Woods entrance, take the Main Trail of the park up the
right side of Redwood Creek past magnificent redwoods.
0.2 Junction. Take the signed Panoramic Trail right for a long steady
climb. In February, look for pink trillium and blue hound's tongue
among the ferns, tanoak and redwoods.
0.5 Ravine. About 100 yds past the first ravine, notice the two similar
small trees, both with light-green fuzzy leaves; ocean spray on the left
and California hazel on the right side of the trail.
1.5 Junction with Lost Trail. Stay right and continue uphill. Look for
red Indian warrior, white zigadene, blue larkspur and iris in spring.
Ahead, Spanish broom produces a fragrant yellow flower.
1.8 Junction and highway. Take the signed Panoramic Trail right.
(The Panoramic Trail formerly was called the Ocean View Trail.)
2.1 Junction. Bear right, downhill on the signed Redwood Trail.
2.4 Bench. Here is a good spot to enjoy the views across Muir
Woods to the ocean. Notice the young Douglas firs about to
overgrow the chaparral. In spring, look for yellow monkeyflower, tree
poppy, red Indian paintbrush and pink chaparral pea.
2.8 Junction with the Tourist Club. This club was founded in 1912 by
German immigrants as a branch of a European hiking club. Continue
above the club to the road and bear left 100' to the signed Sun Trail.
2.9 Sun Trail. The Sun Trail earns its name by skirting the southwest-
facing hillside overlooking Muir Woods. Wildflowers begin in February
building to a peak in April with white zigadene, yellow buttercup,
poppy, broom, blue-eyed grass, lupine, blue dicks, pink
checkerbloom and paintbrush providing great color.
3.5 Junction. Follow the signed Dipsea Trail right as it drops steeply
down the hillside, crossing the highway, into a bay-filled ravine. After
two or more years of greater than normal rainfall, these bays suffer a
blight, losing many leaves, but generally survive.
4.2 Parking lot, snack shop, gift shop and restroom facilities.

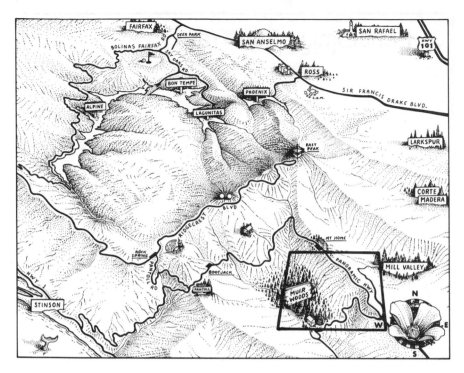

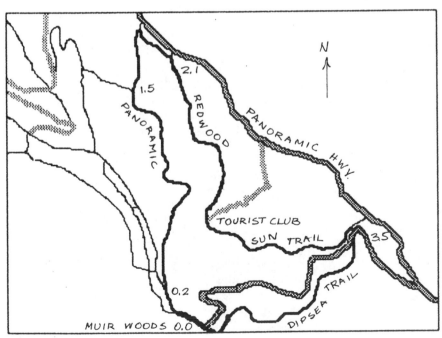

4 Muir Woods - TCC - Dipsea Trails

Distance: 6.3 miles
Elevation Change: 1200'
Rating: Hiking - 10   Running - 7
When to Go: Good anytime, best in April when the bridge is open.
A dramatic hike into deep redwood forest with plunging creek, down
an open ridge with views and flowers, then into a lush canyon.

0.0 Start at the Muir Woods parking lot. Check at the kiosk to see if
the Dipsea Trail bridge is open. Follow the Main Trail along the right
side of Redwood Creek. The trail has several nature information signs
describing the redwood forest.
0.9 Junction. Take the signed Bootjack Trail along the right side of
Redwood Creek. Notice the light green leaves of western azalea,
hazel and big leaf maple against the dark green redwood needles.
1.3 Slides. Downed trees and large boulders testify to the creek's
stormy winters. Look for white milkmaids, pink sorrel, wood rose,
trillium and pink clintonia along the mossy trail.
2.3 Van Wyck Meadow and two junctions. Continue past the first
junction and take the signed TCC Trail left over the creek. Blue
hound's tongue joins other redwood dwellers along the path.
2.8 Manzanita. Notice the dead manzanita from an old chaparral
community. Now, bay, ferns and huckleberry lie under the conifers.
3.7 Two junctions. First go left, then right to take the signed TCC
Trail towards the Dipsea Trail.
4.1 Junction. Eventually, we'll take the Dipsea Trail left down to Muir
Woods. However, now go right, uphill 200' to the hilltop for great
views and wildflowers. This hilltop is known as "Cardiac Hill" to the
1500 Dipsea runners who struggle up from Muir Woods each June.
Now backtrack down the trail and follow the Dipsea Trail to the road.
Watch for red columbine along the road in late spring.
4.5 Junction. Leave the road and go right down the Dipsea Trail.
4.7 Open hillside. This meadow is called "The Hogsback" by Dipsea
runners. It is said to be where the race is won or lost.
5.9 Junction. Take the trail left, down into a moist canyon filled with
bay, hazel, berries and ferns. If the bridge is out, take the road.
6.2 Bridge. Cross the creek under red alders and head left. On the
path, notice the buckeye tree tangled in its own branches.
6.3 Back at Muir Woods with full facilities, but limited parking.

13

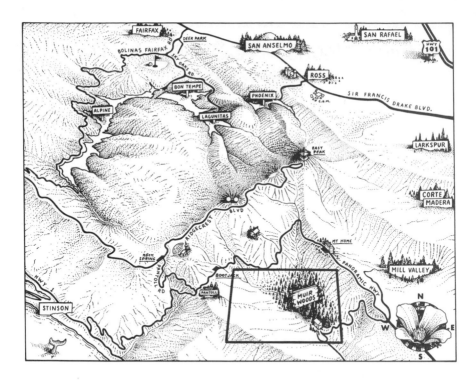

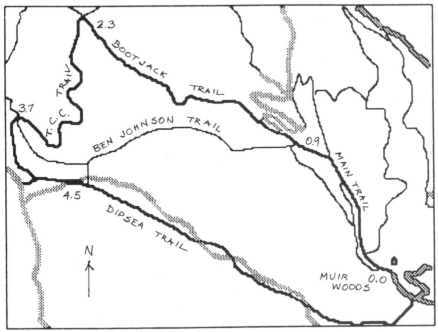

5 Panoramic - Lost - Sierra Trails

Distance: 3.4 miles
Elevation Change: 600'
Rating: Hiking - 9   Running - 5
When to Go: Good anytime, best January to March.
This is a great hike that descends steeply to Fern Creek, then
gradually climbs back through chaparral and redwoods.

0.0 From the north end of the parking lot opposite Mt Home, take the
signed Trestle Trail. In early spring, look for red Indian warrior, purple
mission bells and iris along the stairs. At the road, head left past
manzanita and chamise.
0.2 Gate and junction. Take the signed Panoramic Trail right past
broom and other non-native plants. Good views towards the ocean.
0.4 Junction. Follow the Panoramic Trail (originally called the Ocean
View Trail) right towards Muir Woods. Flowers starting in February
include white zigadene and blue hound's tongue. Up ahead, Douglas
fir has invaded a chaparral area.
0.7 Junction. At the redwood grove, take the Lost Trail right. This
trail was constructed by members of the Tourist Club in 1914. It is very
steep in places and was blocked for a long time by a massive slide in
the 1930's.
1.3 Junction and bridge. Bear right down the picturesque 50 foot
bridge and continue upstream along the left bank. The hike came
steeply down the south-facing hill through Douglas fir and bay. Now it
climbs the north-facing hill more gradually through redwoods, pink
trillium and clintonia. Notice how many redwoods are burned on the
uphill side where forest debris or duff collects.
1.9 Plevin-Cut and Camp Alice Eastwood junctions. At the first
junction, continue right. At Camp Alice Eastwood, go right across the
parking circle and take the signed Sierra Trail up the dirt road.
2.0 Water tank. At the water tank and bench, the road abruptly ends
and a trail swings in and out of a transition zone between two unlikely
bedfellows, redwood and chaparral.
2.5 Chinquapin. Look for a small grove of golden chinquapin with
2-inch leaves, green on top and gold underneath.
2.6 Junction. Head right on the Troop 80 Trail towards Mt Home.
3.0 Fern Creek and junction. Go left on the paved road.
3.4 Stairs. Take the stairs back up to the parking area.

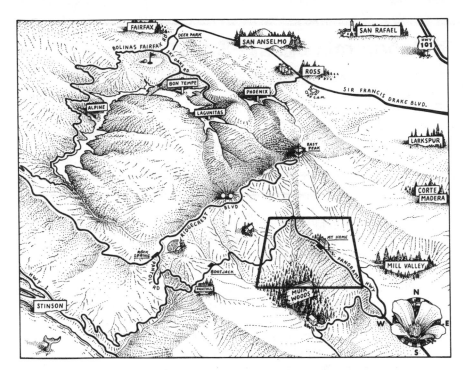

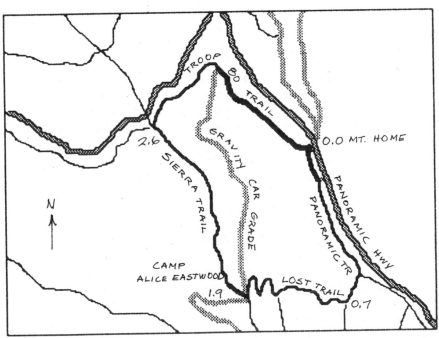

6 Troop 80 - Matt Davis Trails

Distance: 5.0 miles
Elevation Change: 550'
Rating: Hiking - 9   Running - 6
When to Go: Good all year, best in winter and spring.
A great hike through redwood canyons, over cascading creeks, then up into a mixture of forest and chaparral with good views south.

0.0 From the north end of the parking lot opposite Mt Home, take the signed Trestle Trail. In spring, look for red Indian warrior, purple mission bells and iris along the stairs, and red paintbrush, yellow monkeyflower, blue ceanothus and lupine down along the road.
0.5 Junction. Take the signed Troop 80 Trail up the stairs past ferns, moss, tanoak, huckleberry and redwoods. This trail was built in 1931 by the Ingleside, San Francisco Boy Scout Troop.
0.8 Junction and bridge. Continue right at the junction, then enter a small arbor of chinquapin with slim, green-gold leaves. Ahead, good views and in May, white calochortus.
1.7 Junction. On the left is the WW 1 Memorial Tree. Continue straight to Van Wyck Meadow. The meadow, originally called Lower Rattlesnake Camp, was renamed for Sidney M. Van Wyck, president of the TCC in 1920-21 and active in creating Mt Tamalpais State Park.
1.8 Two junctions and Van Wyck Meadow. Take the signed Bootjack Trail right. Look for yellow buttercup, poppy and blue-eyed grass.
1.9 Junction with Alpine Trail. Continue the steep ascent towards Bootjack, passing over small bridges and under large redwoods.
2.3 Bootjack. Cross Panoramic highway and bear right. Go through the picnic area and take the signed Matt Davis Trail towards the Mt Home. The trail starts out level through a mixture of forest and chaparral, then makes several short rocky descents. Good views.
2.8 Bridge. Just past the bridge, look for California nutmeg with sharp green 1-inch needles. Ahead, monkeyflower has colonized a controlled burn area while burned chamise make a comeback.
3.6 Junction with Nora Trail. Continue right towards the Mt Home, past the unlikely combination of chaparral and dense redwoods.
4.2 Waterfalls and junction. A little beyond Fern Canyon with two winter waterfalls, bear right at the junction onto the old railroad bed. Continue towards the signed Mt Home.
5.0 Back at the parking lot. Water and restroom facilities.

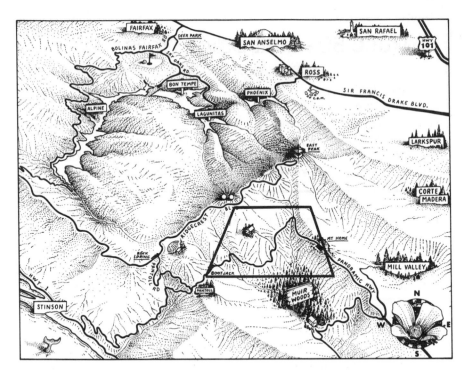

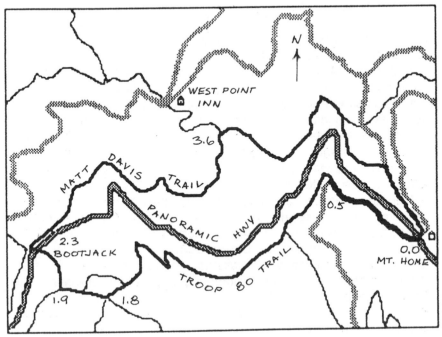

7 Matt Davis Trail - Old RR Grade

Distance: 5.2 miles
Elevation Change: 800'
Rating: Hiking - 8   Running - 8
When to go: Best on a clear day in fall, winter or spring.
A good hike past chaparral and redwood ravines to West Point Inn,
then back through history along the Old RR Grade. Great views.

0.0 Start at the parking lot opposite Mt Home. Cross the highway and take the paved road up past the Fire Station. Continue through the gate towards the water tank. Chaparral includes chamise, manzanita, ceanothus, yerba santa and chaparral pea.

0.3 Junction. Past two water tanks, take the signed Matt Davis Trail left. Called "The dean of the trail workers", Matt Davis lived and worked on the mountain until his death in 1938.

0.7 Junction. Bear left towards the bridge over Fern Creek. Look for white modesty, zigadene, yellow monkeyflower, red paintbrush and iris along the trail. Ahead, the hike passes the first of a dozen stands of dense redwoods. Good views in chaparral areas.

1.4 Junction and bridge. Take the signed Nora Trail up the right side of the creek. Look for slim Solomon and elk clover under the redwoods. Up ahead the trail crosses a bridge to continue uphill.

1.9 West Point Inn. This historic railroad tavern, built in 1904, was a connecting point for the Bolinas Stage. Water, restrooms and beverages available on weekends and most afternoons. During spring and summer, a pancake breakfast is served once a month. To continue the hike, take the first road right downhill. The Old Railroad Grade winds down the mountain through chaparral, in and out of wooded ravines, and never at a grade steeper than seven percent.

2.7 Fern Creek waterfall. Climb the stairs for a refreshing rest.

3.2 Junction with Throckmorton Rd. Continue left around the ridge into more luxuriant growth. Up ahead, you can see part of the Double Bow Knot that helped create the "Crookedest Railroad in the World."

3.8 Junction. Bear right to enter the Double Bow Knot.

4.1 Junction. Keep right again past the non-native conifers.

4.2 Mesa Station. A loading platform is all that remains of Mesa Station. Up ahead, continue right past invasive French broom.

5.1 Junction. Continue left here and right ahead towards Mt Home.

5.2 Back at Mt Home with water, restroom and restaurant.

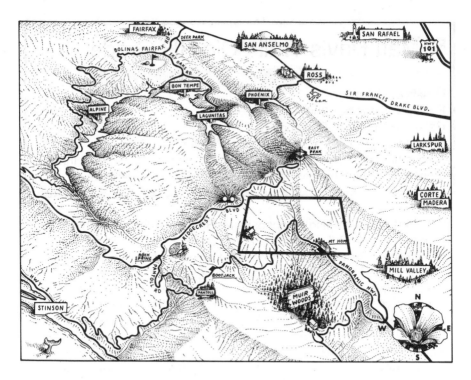

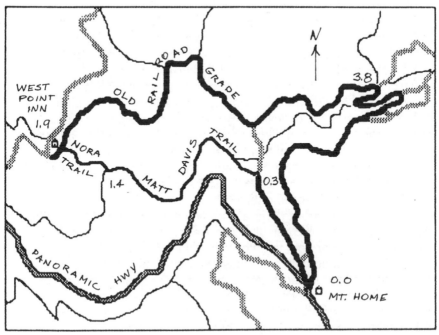

8 TCC - Alpine Trails

Distance: 3.6 miles
Elevation Change: 500'
Rating: Hiking - 9   Running - 9
When to Go: Good anytime, best in early spring.
This is a good hike exploring the dense woods east of Pantoll.
Cardiac Hill on the Dipsea Trail provides vistas and wildflowers.

0.0 Start at the Bootjack parking lot. Cross the highway and take the signed Bootjack Trail towards Van Wyck Meadow. The trail drops steeply down past Douglas fir and bay into redwood forest. In early spring, look for white milkmaids, blue-eyed grass and iris.
0.2 Junction with Alpine Trail. Bear left to cross two small bridges ahead. Watch for white fairy bells and pink trillium.
0.4 Junction. Just past the bench and western azalea, continue right on the Bootjack Trail. The trail goes alongside moss-covered boulders, then down past a large red-brown vertical sandstone slab.
0.5 Junction and Van Wyck Meadow. Take the signed TCC Trail right, across the creek and into redwoods. The TCC Trail was built in 1918 and named for the Tamalpais Conservation Club, often called the "Guardians of the Mountain" for their conservation activities.
1.0 Manzanita. Notice the dead manzanita from an old chaparral community. Now, bay, ferns and huckleberry lie under the conifers.
1.9 Two junctions. First go left, then right to take the signed TCC Trail towards the Dipsea Trail.
2.3 Junction. Take the Dipsea Trail right uphill.
2.4 Junction and hill. Congratulations! You have climbed "Cardiac Hill", as it's called by the throng of Dipsea runners who climb 1200 feet out of Muir Woods each June. Views and wildflowers, including yellow buttercup, poppy, blue-eyed grass, blue dicks and pink checkerbloom. Go right on the road.
2.5 Junction with Old Mine Rd. Bear right into Douglas fir and bay.
2.7 Junction. Take the Old Mine Trail right. Up ahead, an 1863 mining claim was staked out hoping to find gold and silver.
3.0 Junction and Pantoll. Water, tables and restrooms. Continue past the Ranger Station and take the signed Alpine Trail just before the highway. The trail follows the road downhill.
3.4 Junction. Take the signed Bootjack Trail left.
3.6 Back at Bootjack with water, tables and restroom.

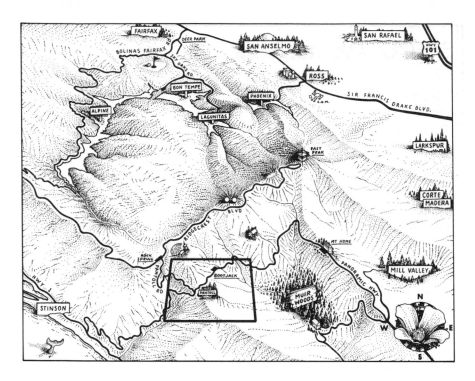

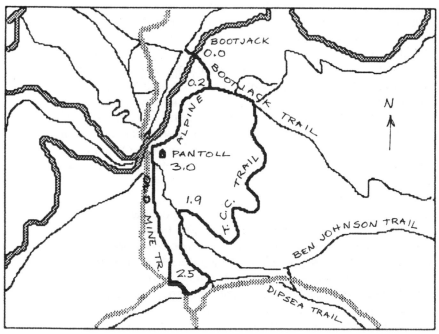

9 Bootjack - Rock Spring Trails

Distance: 4.1 miles
Elevation Change: 600'
Rating: Hiking - 8   Running - 7
When to Go: Good any cool, clear day, best February to April.
This is a good sunshine hike mostly through chaparral, first climbing to the Mountain Theater, then to West Point Inn and back.

0.0 Start at the Bootjack parking lot. Take the signed Bootjack Trail towards Mt Theater. Beyond the picnic area, two trails start uphill. Take the right trail and climb into oak-bay woodland.
0.2 Junction with Old Stage Rd. Go left on the road 20 feet, then right 20 feet, then left to continue on the Bootjack Trail. In early spring, look for blue hound's tongue, white milkmaids and iris.
0.7 Junction and Mt Theater. Turn right at the Pantoll Jct and head to the top of the theater to enjoy a unique setting. This natural amphitheater has been the site of spring plays since 1913. The present theater was built in 1934 using over 40,000 stones, some weighing over 4000 lbs. Each stone is buried so that only a small fraction is visible. Water and restrooms nearby. To continue the hike, head to the top northeast corner of the theater.
0.8 Junction. Take the Rock Spring Trail towards West Point Inn. This south-facing trail gradually descends through chaparral and wooded ravines. Watch for yellow monkeyflower, tree poppy, blue-eyed grass, white calochortus and red Indian warrior.
1.4 Rocky knoll. Great views to San Francisco and the East Bay.
2.3 West Point Inn. Water, restrooms and beverages on weekends and most afternoons. Pancakes once a month from May to September. A glorious setting. To continue the hike, take the signed Nora Trail in front of the picnic area.
2.8 Junction. Take the Matt Davis Trail right over the bridge, out of the redwoods, and into a mixture of oak, huckleberry, manzanita, chamise with occasional Douglas fir and bay trees.
3.3 Controlled burn area. The first of several controlled burn areas. Notice chamise resprouting from the burl at the base of the dead wood. Monkeyflower is widespread.
3.7 Bridge. The trail enters a ravine, crosses a bridge on Rattlesnake Creek, then goes up a rocky slope.
4.1 Back at Bootjack picnic area.

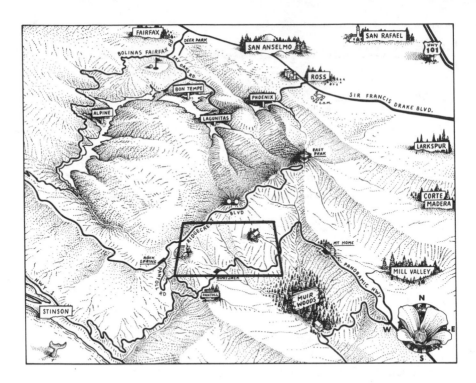

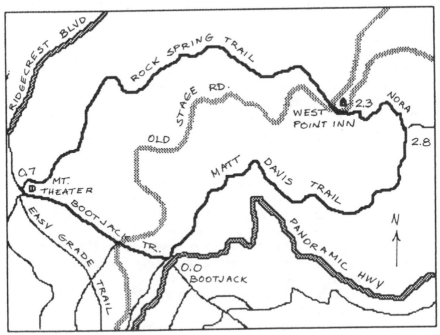

10 Easy Grade to Mountain Theater

Distance: 2.2 miles
Elevation Change: 500'
Rating: Hiking - 10   Running - 9
When to Go: Good any clear day, best in spring.
This short hike climbs from Pantoll through forest to the Mt Theater,
then over open hills with magnificent views south and east.

0.0 Start at the Pantoll parking lot. Cross the highway, bear right and
go along the paved road signed to East Peak on the Old Railroad
Grade. Watch for yellow buttercup, poppies and blue-eyed grass.
Continue on the road past two junctions.
0.1 Junction. Take the signed Easy Grade Trail left towards the Mt
Theater. The trail climbs into wooded hills with views east framed by
Douglas fir, oak and bay trees.
0.3 Junction with Easy Grade Spur Trail. Keep left at the Spur Trail
and straight up ahead. Watch for white milkmaids and iris.
0.4 Junction with Riding and Hiking Trail. Continue straight.
0.8 Mt Theater. This natural amphitheater has been the site of spring
plays since 1913. The present theater was built in 1934 using over
40,000 stones, some weighing over 4000 lbs. Each stone is buried
so that only a small fraction is visible. Water and restrooms nearby. To
continue the hike, head up the right side of the theater, then back
across the top and admire the views of the theater nestled in the
trees. Continue west on the road.
1.0 Junction. Head left on the signed road to Madrone Grove and
explore the hilltop covered with large madrone, oak and Douglas fir
trees. To continue the hike, backtrack, go through the gate, cross the
highway and pick up the signed trail towards Rock Spring.
1.2 Rock Spring. From the parking area, cross the highway, bear left
and take the signed Mt Theater Fire Trail uphill.
1.3 Junction with Old Mine Trail. Turn right and follow the trail in
open hillside with blue lupine and pink filaree.
1.5 Spectacular views. This rocky knoll provides one of the finest
views in the world. The trail now drops steeply into an interesting
oak -bay forest with occasional views.
1.9 Junction. Continue straight ahead towards Pantoll and up ahead
at the paved road, bear right.
2.2 Back at Pantoll Ranger Station. Full facilities.

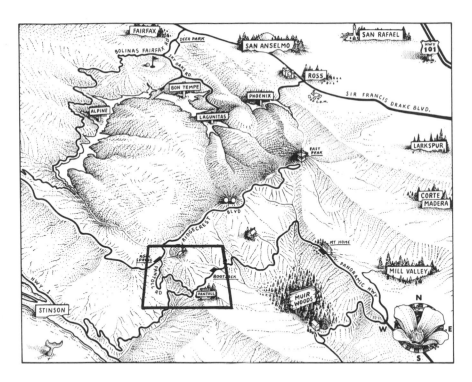

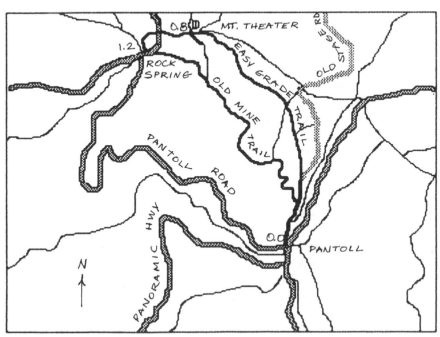

12 Coastal - Cataract Trails

Distance: 6.6 miles
Elevation Change: 400', then 300'
Rating: Hiking - 10   Running - 6
When to Go: Not summer, best on a clear day in March or April
Here is a magnificent hike through dense forest, past flowering hill-
sides, then along a refreshing creek. Spectacular views.

0.0 From the Pantoll parking lot, cross Panoramic Hwy and take the
Pantoll road 200' uphill to the signed Matt Davis Trail towards Stinson
Beach. The trail starts out along open hillside, but soon enters dense
woods of Douglas fir, oak and bay. Wildflowers along the trail include
white zigadene, yellow poppy, calochortus, blue hound's tongue,
blue-eyed grass, blue dicks and iris.
1.2 Open hillside. Leaving the woods, look for white popcorn flower,
yellow buttercup, pink checkerbloom and lupine. Great views. Up
ahead, a short spur trail leads left to a lookout point.
1.6 Junction. Stay right to climb gently on the Coastal Trail. In
summer, thistles and stickers crowd this hillside trail.
2.4 Rock outcroppings. Green-grey lichen enjoy the cool and moist
coastal climate on these small rocky patches.
3.3 Road junction. Turn right on the dirt road, climb the first knoll,
then take the short trail left up to Ridgecrest Blvd.
3.5 Highway junction. Continue on the dirt road to Laurel Dell.
3.8 Junction. A trail leads right, over the bridge on Cataract Creek.
Go left on Cataract Trail through the meadow to Laurel Dell.
4.1 Laurel Dell picnic area. Continue north on Cataract Trail.
4.2 Waterfalls. Beneath a big leaf maple, moss-covered rocks and
ferns, Cataract Creek starts its vigorous plunge to Alpine Lake. To
continue the hike, backtrack south and stay on the left side of Cataract
Creek all the way up to Rock Spring.
4.7 Ledge. The trail hugs a hillside on a ledge overlooking large
rocks and large trees washed into the creek. Lots of huckleberry, iris,
ferns and moss lie witness to the creek's annual rampage.
5.6 Rock Spring. Cross the highway, bear left and take the signed Mt
Theater Fire Trail uphill, then right on the Old Mine Trail.
5.9 Spectacular views. This rocky knoll provides one of the finest
views in the world. Good picnic spot if it's not too windy.
6.6 Back at Pantoll Ranger Station. Full facilities.

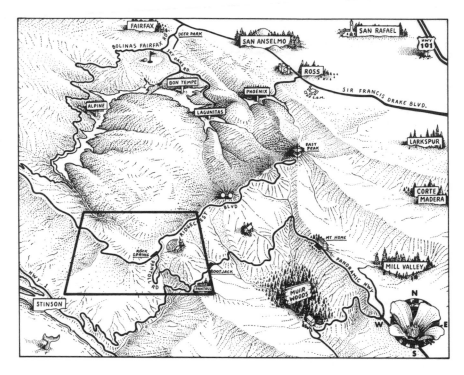

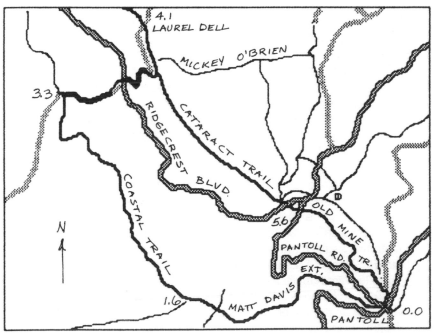

13 Simmons - Cataract Trails

Distance: 3.2 miles
Elevation Change: 450'
Rating: Hiking - 10   Running - 3
When to Go: Good anytime, best in winter and spring.
A great hike through woods and chaparral to Barth's Retreat, then
along two wild and wooded creeks.

0.0 Start at the Rock Spring parking area. Take the trail down the left
side of the meadow and follow the signed Benstein Trail. Search for
woodpeckers in the stumps ahead and for yellow buttercup, gold
fields, poppy and blue-eyed grass in the meadow.
0.2 Junction. Bear left on the Simmons Trail. Ahead, the trail enters
a ravine with redwoods and iris, then crosses a bridge.
0.3 Junction. The trail leaves the creek and climbs steeply onto a
hilltop covered with tanoak and large Douglas fir trees.
0.4 Chaparral. The trail abruptly leaves the forest and enters a rocky
chaparral slope with white zigadene and calochortus. Head north
towards Sargent cypress growing on serpentine soil.
1.0 Barth's Retreat and junction. The trail drops down through
Douglas fir, bay, oak and madrone to cross a creek to Barth's Retreat.
Emil Barth, pianist and avid hiker from 1886, built his camp in the
1920's. Water, picnic tables and restroom are nearby. To continue the
hike, take the Mickey O'Brien Trail, which stays on the left side of
Barth's Creek, all the way down to Laurel Dell.
1.4 Tall oak. A tall oak rests a tired branch on a 20' rock lying along
the trail. Opposite, a madrone leans against a Douglas fir tree.
1.6 Junction with Cataract Trail. Go right towards Laurel Dell. Look
for yellow buttercup, pink shooting star and checkerbloom.
1.7 Laurel Dell picnic area with water, tables and restroom. From the
picnic area, take the signed Cataract Trail downstream.
1.8 Waterfalls. Here, Cataract Creek starts its cascading plunge
towards Alpine Lake. To continue the hike, backtrack upstream and
take Cataract Trail along the left side of the meadow.
2.4 Ledge. The trail hugs a hillside on a ledge overlooking large
rocks and large trees washed into the creek. Lots of huckleberry, iris,
ferns and moss lie witness to the creek's annual rampage.
3.1 Junction and small bridge. Bear left into the meadow.
3.2 Parking area. Ocean view, tables and restroom.

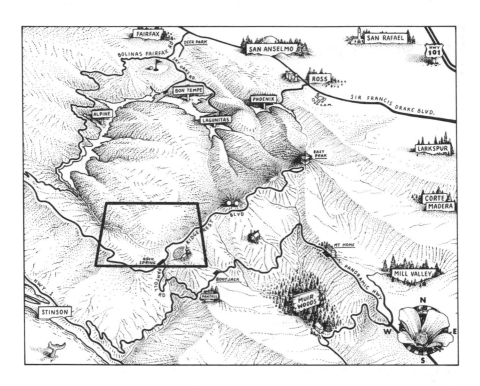

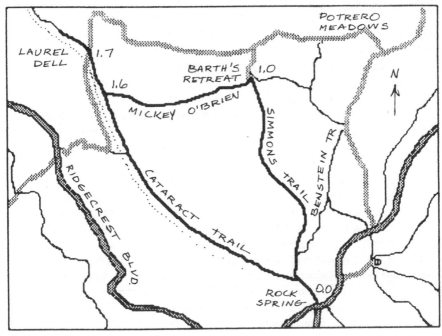

14 Potrero Meadows - Laurel Dell

Distance: 4.2 miles
Elevation Change: 450'
Rating: Hiking - 8   Running - 4
When to Go: Good anytime, best in winter and spring.
A grand hike through mixed forest to Potrero Meadows, along a road to Laurel Dell, then returning along scenic Cataract Creek.

0.0 Start at the Rock Spring parking area. Take the trail down the left side of the meadow and follow the signed Benstein Trail. Search for woodpeckers in the stumps ahead and for yellow buttercup, gold fields, poppy and blue-eyed grass in the meadow.
0.2 Junction. Take the signed Benstein Trail right into Douglas fir and tanoak trees and up past moss-covered rocks. Look for white milkmaids, blue hound's tongue, mission bells and iris in spring.
0.4 Junction. Continue left towards signed Potrero Meadows.
0.7 Junction. Go left on the Rock Spring - Lagunitas Rd.
0.8 Junction. Take the signed Benstein Trail left into woods.
1.0 Ocean view. A short spur trail leads to views west.
1.1 Golden chinquapin. The trail enters a small forest of chinquapin with narrow leaves, green on top and gold underneath.
1.2 Junction. Head righ, or north, into chaparral, then down serpentine rocks past a stand of Sargent cypress.
1.3 Junction with Laurel Dell road. Cross the road and continue down to Potrero Meadows. Picnic table, barbecue, hitching post, restroom facilities and western azalea, that blooms in May and June. To continue the hike, take the Laurel Dell Rd west into chaparral.
2.7 Laurel Dell picnic area with water, tables and restroom. This area was once a small ranch known as Old Stove Camp. From the picnic area, take the signed Cataract Trail downstream.
2.8 Waterfalls. Here, Cataract Creek starts its cascading plunge towards Alpine Lake. To continue the hike, backtrack upstream and take the trail along the left side of the meadow. Spring flowers include yellow buttercup, pink shooting star and baby-blue eyes.
3.0 Junction. At the end of the meadow, bear right as the trail stays along the left side of Cataract Creek. Lots of iris, ferns and moss lie under oak, bay and Douglas fir in a riparian setting.
4.1 Junction and small bridge. Bear left into another meadow.
4.2 Parking area. Ocean view, tables and restroom.

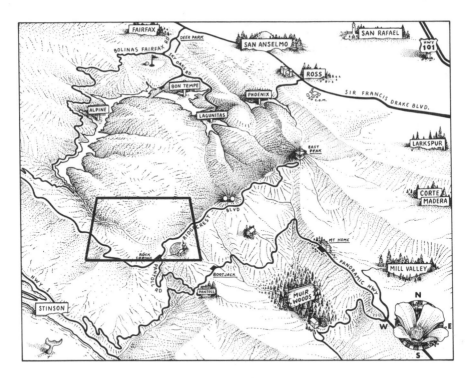

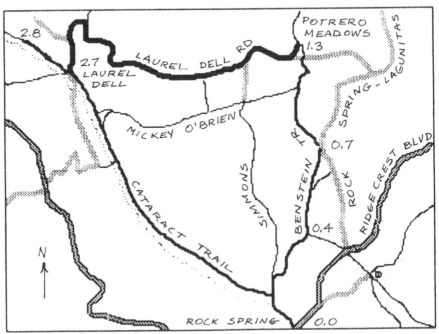

15 Benstein - International Trails

Distance: 4.9 miles
Elevation Change: 600'
Rating: Hiking - 8   Running - 6
When to Go: Good on any cool, clear day, best in spring.
This is a good hike that goes on both sides of the mountain through woods, chaparral and wildflowers; great views.

0.0 Start at the Rock Spring parking area. Take the trail down the left side of the meadow and follow the signed Benstein Trail. Search for woodpeckers in the stumps ahead and for yellow buttercup, gold fields, poppy and blue-eyed grass in the meadow.
0.2 Junction. Take the signed Benstein Trail right into Douglas fir and tanoak trees and up past moss-covered rocks. Look for white milkmaids, blue hound's tongue, mission bells and iris in spring.
0.4 Junction. Continue left towards signed Potrero Meadows.
0.7 Junction. Go left on the Rock Spring - Lagunitas Rd.
1.1 Junction and meadow. Stay right and follow the road around the edge of Potrero Meadows, skirting a Douglas fir forest.
1.3 Junction and Rifle Camp. Go down through the picnic area, cross the creek and take the signed Northside Trail into woods. Up ahead, watch for white zigadene and calochortus in the chaparral.
1.8 Views. Great views north, east and west. Continue straight across the serpentine ridgeline; notice the stunted Sargent cypress.
1.9 Junction. Take the signed International Trail right. Notice the manzanita being succeeded by Douglas fir, oak and some nutmeg.
2.4 Junction with Ridgecrest Blvd. Cross the road and take the Miller Trail down the rocky hillside past chamise, manzanita, ceanothus, yerba santa, yellow monkeyflower and red Indian paintbrush. John Miller, who worked on trails for over 30 years, was injured while working here in 1947 at the age of 80.
2.7 Junction. Turn right and take the Old RR Grade downhill.
3.1 Junction and West Point Inn. Water, restroom, tables and view anytime, beverages on weekends and most afternoons. To continue the hike, take the Rock Spring Trail behind the Inn.
4.6 Mountain Theater. Water, restroom and picnic area. Continue right, around the top of the Theater, and along the paved path to the highway. Cross the road and take the trail to Rock Spring.
4.9 Rock Spring parking area. Ocean view, table and restroom.

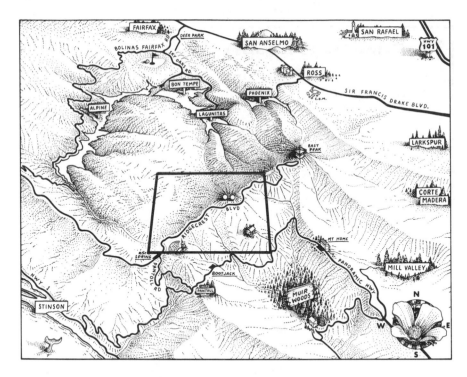

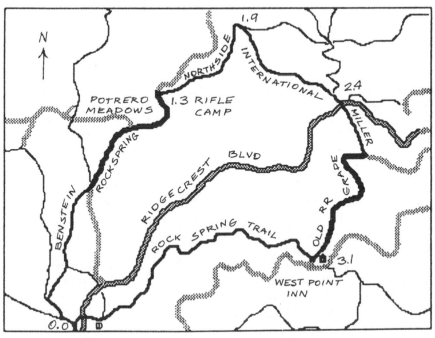

16 East Peak Loop Trail

Distance: 0.7 miles
Elevation Change: 50'
Rating: Hiking - 10   Running - 10
When to go: Great anytime on a clear windless day.
This short hike on paved path offers incomparable views of the San Francisco Bay Area. The flora is primarily chaparral.

0.0 From the East Peak parking lot, go east towards the restroom and take the signed Verna Dunshee Trail to circle the peak counterclockwise. The hike begins with great views of Southern Marin, San Francisco and the coast. Follow the path into the chaparral community of oak, manzanita and chamise. Also look for yerba santa, a shrub with dark green, sticky bay-shaped leaves and white flowers in spring. Other flowers on the hike include white milkmaids, modesty, yellow monkeyflower, red Indian paintbrush, pitcher sage, chaparral pea and blue lupine.

0.1 View. Look down at Mesa junction due south. Here you can see the Old Railroad Grade make its famous Double Bow Knot, and laying claim to the "Crookedest Railroad in the World."

0.2 Sunrise Point. On a clear day, this point offers one of the finest views in the world! Watch for turkey vultures soaring below you.

0.3 Junction and bench. Continue on the paved path. Sometimes you can see mountain climbers practicing their skills on the jagged rocks above you. Up ahead, just before the second wooden bridge, see if you can find bush chinquapin, a small shrub with a prickly bur and bay-like leaves, green on top, gold underneath, struggling for existence in the dry rocky soil.

0.4 Junction and bend. The trail down to North Knee is rocky and narrow. Continue on the path round a bend opening up great vistas north. Vegetation here is more robust than on the south side.

0.5 Lakes. Good views of Bon Tempe and Lagunitas lakes and the hills of north Marin. On a crystal-clear day, you can see the geysers of Sonoma county puffing away.

0.6 Rocks. The red-brown rock outcroppings most common along the path are quartz - tourmaline. Inspect the various colored lichens making these rocks their home.

0.7 Parking area with tables, water, restroom and a small visitor center that is open on weekends.

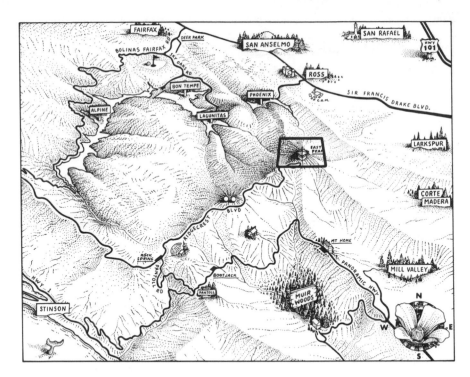

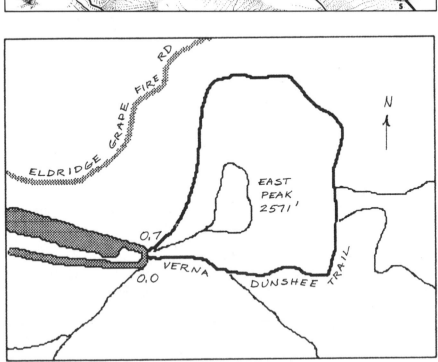

17 North Side Trail

Distance: 4.2 miles
Elevation Change: 500'
Rating: Hiking - 8   Running - 2
When to go: Good anytime, best March to May after rain.
Wear sturdy boots to hike the rocky north slopes below East Peak.
Good chaparral, some redwoods and lots of oak and nutmeg.

0.0 From the East Peak parking lot, take the one-way paved road west, away from the facilities. Good views over the chaparral.
0.3 Junction with Eldridge Grade. Go through the gate and downhill past oak, chamise, manzanita, ceanothus, yerba santa and occasional chaparral pea. Wildflowers along the road include white milkmaids, modesty, yellow monkeyflower, red Indian warrior, Indian paintbrush and iris. Watch for California nutmeg, a yew with flat, one-inch sharp green needles, common on this hike.
0.6 Junction. Continue on the road right. Good views east.
1.0 Hairpin turn. Continue around the hairpin turn. Up ahead, more moisture and better soil produce more luxuriant growth.
1.3 Junction. Take the signed road left toward Colier Spring.
1.4 Inspiration Point and junction. Great views in all directions. The hike leaves the road here and follows the narrow North Side Trail, which starts out level and heads southwest into the canyon below East Peak. Lots of white zigadene here and dense oak, bay, madrone and California nutmeg trees ahead.
2.8 Two springs. A small spring supports western azalea, while just ahead, another spring provides water for a redwood grove.
3.1 Colier Spring Jct. Pause at the bench just below the spring to enjoy the large redwood grove. Alice Eastwood called this spring "Butterfly Spring" because of the many specimens she found here. To continue the hike, take the signed Colier Trail, first left, uphill along the winter streambed. The trail climbs steeply through oak, bay, madrone and nutmeg, but no redwoods.
3.4 Two junctions. Go left up to the highway, then head east 100' to pick up the Lakeview Trail which climbs toward Middle Peak.
3.6 Junction. Continue downhill on the road. On a clear day, you can see northwest to Tomales Bay at the end of Bolinas Ridge.
3.9 Junction. Follow the highway left up to the parking area.
4.2 Back at the parking area with water, tables and restrooms.

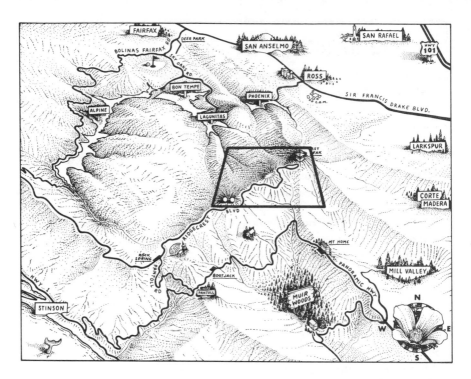

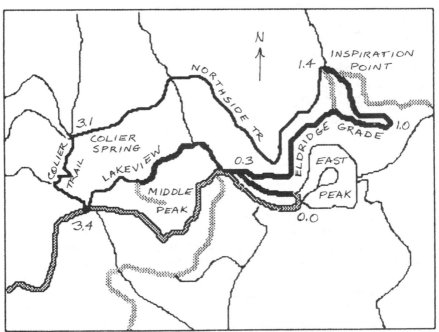

18 Phoenix Lake Trail

Distance: 2.6 miles
Elevation Change: 200'
Rating: Hiking - 7   Running - 10
When to Go: Good November to May, best February to April.
This is a good hike around the lake through a mixture of oak, bay and redwood trees with good lakeside views.

0.0 Start at Natalie Greene Park in Ross. Notice the massive slide that occurred in 1986. From the parking lot, take the road uphill past oak, bay and madrone. In spring, look for white wild onion, yellow buttercup, and iris. Watch out for poison oak.

0.3 Dam. Go left to circle the lake clockwise. The milky-green color of the water is due to algae and sediment, both of which are removed when the water is used for drinking. Ahead, yellow monkeyflower, blue brodiaea and red clarkia dot the bank in May and June.

0.9 Junction. Turn right and take the signed Phoenix Trail up the stairs. The trail passes through a mixture of tall oak, bay, Douglas fir and madrone trees shading low growing tanoak and fuzzy-leafed hazel. Pink trillium, white milkmaids and blue hound's tongue bloom in February and March.

1.2 Ravine. After passing under a large red-barked madrone, the trail enters a small ravine. Ferns, pink shooting star, and lush moss cover the left bank in early spring.

1.4 Junction. The stairs down to the right can be used as a shortcut in dry times. For a more interesting route, follow the trail left into the redwood ravine. The storm of 1986 scoured the creek bottom lowering the channel by three feet. Upcreek, past mudslides have left lots of debris including large trees.

1.5 Redwoods. Notice the quiet as the trail enters a large redwood grove with tall ferns dotting the hillside.

1.6 Junction. Turn right at the small bridge to take the Phoenix Lake Rd towards the dam. Across from the old ranch site, there are bay trees and two kinds of oaks, coast live oak and California black oak.

2.0 Lichen. Lacy lichen, often mistaken for Spanish moss, hangs like cobwebs on the oaks along the lake, while leafy lichen drapes the trunks.

2.3 Dam. Go left down the road.

2.6 Parking area with water, tables and restroom facilities.

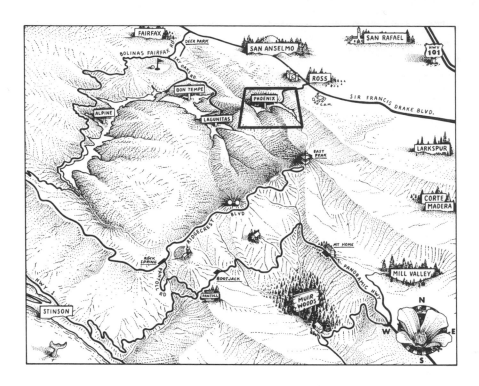

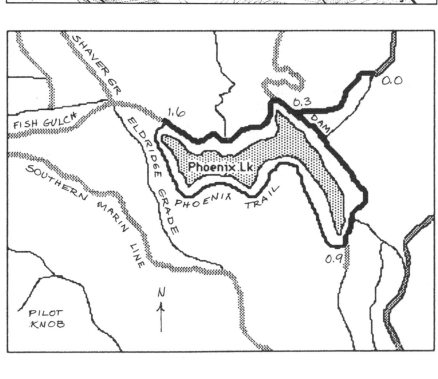

19 Tucker - Bill Williams Trails

Distance: 3.4 miles
Elevation Change: 400'
Rating: Hiking - 8   Running - 9
When to Go: Good anytime, best February through April.
This is a fine hike along the lake, then into two small canyons; first through oak-bay woods, then past redwoods, ferns and mosses.

0.0 Start at Natalie Greene Park in Ross. Notice the massive slide that occurred in 1986. From the parking lot, take the road uphill past oak, bay and madrone. In spring, look for white wild onion, yellow buttercup, and iris. Watch out for poison oak.
0.3 Dam. Go left to circle the lake clockwise. The milky-green color of the water is due to algae and sediment, both of which are removed when the water is used for drinking. Ahead, yellow monkeyflower, blue brodiaea and red clarkia dot the bank in May and June.
0.7 Junction. Turn left onto the signed Allen Trail and head into a small ravine with oak, bay and buckeye trees. Early flowers include pink shooting star, blue hound's tongue, and white zigadene. Later flowers include white modesty, blue dicks and wood rose.
0.9 Junction. The Allen Trail goes left uphill. Stay right and follow the Tucker Trail past mosses, lichens and maidenhair ferns. Several small deer paths cross the trail before the next junction.
1.1 Main canyon. Redwoods grow along the north slope of the Bill Williams canyon. Oaks and bays grow here along the south side. Up ahead, a small dam is just visible down the steep hillside.
1.6 Two junctions. An unmaintained trail comes down from the left. At the second junction, 100 feet ahead, turn right and go steeply down to the creek. Look for mission bells in late winter.
1.7 Two bridges. The trail makes three crossings of the creek; two by bridge and one by foot. (The creek may not be fordable in high water.) Cross the first bridge, go uphill 100 feet to a junction, turn right and go down to the creek for the second crossing by rocks. Walk along the creek past the dam to the second bridge. Cross the creek again and continue along a beautiful trail through the redwoods. Look for white slim Solomon and pink trillium.
2.5 Phoenix Lake Rd. Continue along the lake to the dam.
3.1 Dam. Turn right to take the road down to the parking lot.
3.4 Back at the parking area with water, tables and restrooms.

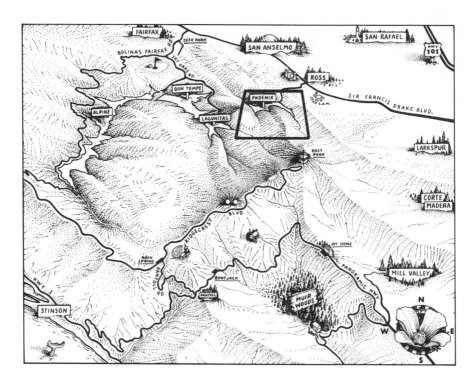

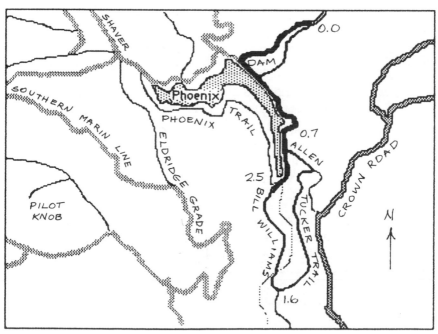

20 Bald Hill Loop

Distance: 3.9 miles
Elevation Change: 1000'
Rating: Hiking - 6   Running - 7
When to Go: Good any cool clear windless day, best in early spring.
Take binoculars and water to make the long climb up the road to Bald
Hill. Spectacular views and good wildflowers.

0.0 Start at Natalie Greene Park in Ross. From the parking lot, take
the road uphill past oak, bay and madrone. Watch for white wild
onion, yellow buttercup, blue forget-me-not, iris, and up by the dam,
crimson clover. Watch out for poison oak.
0.3 Dam. Take the Phoenix Lake Rd to the right.
0.4 Junction. Take the signed Worn Spring Rd right toward Bald Hill.
This road was named after George Austin Worn, descendant of the
family that founded Ross. The road starts under big leaf maple,
buckeye, bay and redwood, then climbs uphill past yellow
monkeyflower, blue hound's tongue and lots of French broom.
0.7 Junction. Go left through the gate and climb steeply.
1.4 Views. Good views south and east. Yellow buttercup, poppy,
white popcorn flower, blue-eyed grass, blue dicks, lupine, and pink
checkerbloom grow along the road from March to May.
2.1 Junction. The road left is the way down. Take the right road 150'
to the top of the hill.
2.2 Bald Hill. Spectacular 360 degree views. Explore the hilltop to
discover the best wildflower display, often yellow gold fields. To
continue the hike, backtrack to the junction and bear right.
2.4 Junction. Bear right to head east. There is a good selection of
wildflowers 100' uphill from this junction. Down the road, coyote
brush and poison oak indicate the coastal scrub community.
2.5 Oaks. Look for two different oaks nearby. The deciduous
California black oak has deeply lobed leaves, 3-4 inches long. The
evergreen coast live oak has one inch leaves with sharp spiny edges.
2.9 Gate. Take the paved road downhill past large estates.
3.2 Junction. Take Upper Road right to Glenwood then right again.
3.6 Junction. Take Lagunitas Road right towards the park. Once
past the park gate, look for blue forget-me-not, white milkmaids,
modesty, woodland star and mission bells in early spring.
3.9 Back at the parking area with water, tables and restrooms.

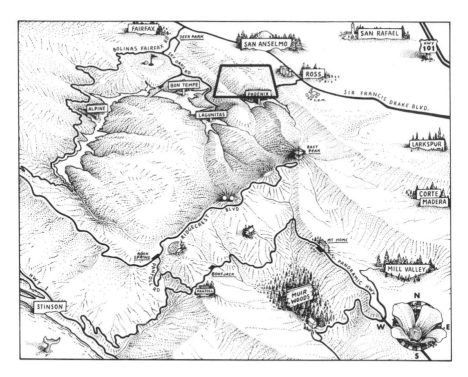

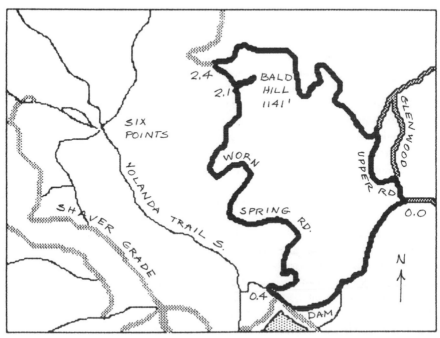

21 Shaver Grade - Yolanda South

Distance: 4.8 miles
Elevation Change: 600'
Rating: Hiking - 9   Running - 9
When to Go: Good November to May, best February to April.
The hike starts with a long steady climb then skirts a south-facing
hillside with good local views and great wildflowers.

0.0 Start at Natalie Greene Park in Ross. Notice the massive slide
that occurred in 1986. From the parking lot, take the road uphill past
oak, bay and madrone. In spring, look for white wild onion, yellow
buttercup, and iris. Watch out for poison oak.
0.3 Dam. Go right on the Phoenix Lake Rd around the lake.
0.7 Junction to Six Pts. This is the trail we'll be returning on.
Continue on the road past the old ranch site.
1.0 Phoenix Jct. Just past the small bridge, take Shaver Grade on
the right up to Five Corners. This is a long steady climb through
changing stands of bay, oak, madrone and redwood. Look for white
milkmaids and blue hound's tongue starting in February.
2.1 Five Corners Jct. Take the road right signed, Yolanda Trail to Six
Pts, and climb steeply. Yolanda once was a small community along
the NWP railroad line between Fairfax and San Anselmo.
2.2 Junction. The first of four small unmarked junctions before Six
Pts. Keep right in each case. A large madrone stands at the hilltop
overlooking Hidden Meadow.
2.6 Junction with Hidden Meadow Trail. Keep left on the road.
2.7 Six Pts Jct. Take the second right, signed Yolanda Trail, towards
Phoenix Lake. Colorful wildflowers and spectacular views ahead as
the trail winds along the south-facing canyon hillside with oaks,
buckeye and chamise.
3.2 Rock slide. A small rock slide caused by one of the many winter
stream beds. Two hundred feet above the slide is Rocky View Pts.
3.3 Wildflowers. Pink shooting stars, blue dicks, yellow poppies, red
larkspur and iris stand guard on small rocky outcroppings.
3.6 View. Spectacular views of Mt Tam.
3.8 Downhill. The trail tumbles downhill past several fallen trees.
Stay right at the small Y-junction ahead.
4.1 Junction. Go left on Phoenix Lake Rd towards the dam.
4.8 Back at the parking lot with tables, water and restrooms.

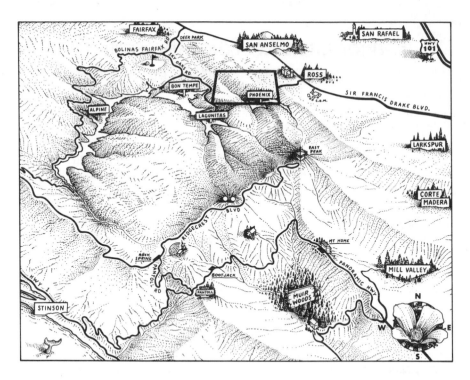

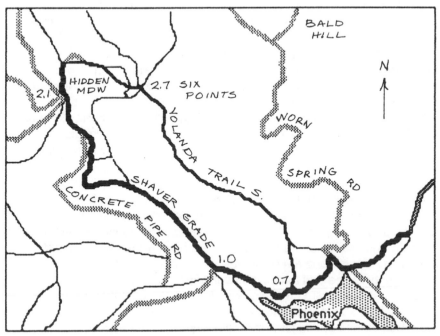

22 Eldridge Grade - Tucker Trail

Distance: 5.2 miles
Elevation Change: 600'
Rating: Hiking - 9   Running - 8
When to Go: Good in winter and spring, best February to April.
Lots of water, views and wildflowers make this a great hike on the
steep north slope of Mt Tam. Sometimes impassable in winter.

0.0 Start at Natalie Greene Park in Ross. From the parking lot, take
the road uphill past oak, bay and madrone. Watch for white wild onion,
yellow buttercup, monkeyflower, iris, and up by the dam, crimson
clover planted for erosion control. Watch out for poison oak.
0.3 Dam. Go right. In April, look for pink Chinese houses.
1.0 Phoenix Jct. Take the first left road, signed Eldridge Grade, for a
steady climb through an interesting combination of redwood, big leaf
maple, oak, bay and madrone. This road was built by John C. Eldridge
in the 1880's as the first wagon road to the summit. It has suffered
many slides and is now being maintained as a trail. Watch for white
modesty, zigadene and blue hound's tongue in February.
1.7 Rock garden. In an open ravine, water streams down large rocks
to nourish mosses, lichens and flowers including red larkspur.
1.8 Junction with Southern Marin Line Rd. Continue left uphill.
2.3 Hairpin junction. Take either road; good views north.
2.8 Junction with the Tucker Trail. As the road curves right, take the
signed Tucker Trail left towards Phoenix Lake.
3.0 Creek. The trail makes a steep descent down the north slope of
Mt Tam past tumbling creeks, cascading waterfalls, western azalea,
redwood and iris; a magnificent hike. Downhill, look for white fairy
bells, pink trillium, star flower and Indian warrior.
3.7 Bill Williams Creek. Cross the creek to head uphill.
3.8 Unmarked junction. Go left, steeply downhill to the bridge.
3.9 Two bridges. The trail makes three crossings of the creek; two by
bridge and one by foot. Cross the first bridge, go uphill 100 feet to a
junction, turn right and go down to the creek for the second crossing
by rocks. Walk along the creek past the dam to the second bridge.
Cross the creek again and continue along the trail.
4.3 Phoenix Lake Rd. In June, look for red clarkia on the bank.
4.9 Dam. Turn right to take the road down to the parking lot.
5.2 Back at the parking lot with tables, water and restrooms.

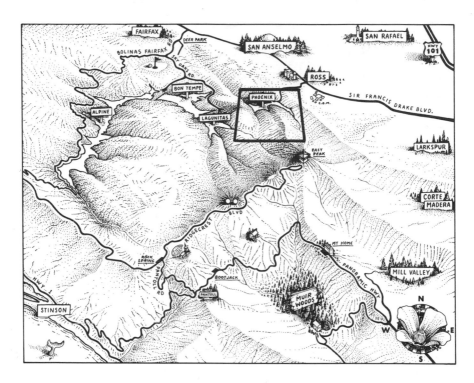

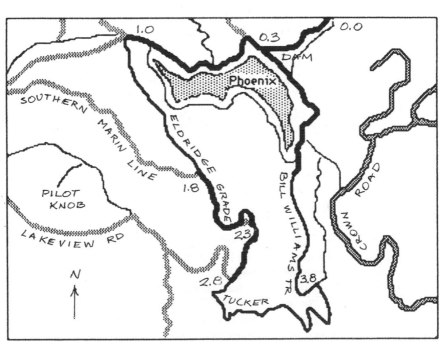

23 Deer Park Rd - Six Pts Trail

Distance: 3.0 miles
Elevation Change: 400'
Rating: Hiking - 8   Running - 9
When to Go: Good November to May, best February through April.
This is a good wildflower hike starting with a long steady climb along
roads, then downhill on a narrow trail through dense forest.

0.0 Start at Deer Park in Fairfax. From the parking area, go left
around the school and through the field. Deer Park Rd begins at the
gate just past a large bay tree and climbs slowly past majestic oaks with
nearby madrone and buckeye trees. Wildflowers along the road
include white milkmaids, slim Solomon, yellow buttercup, blue
hound's tongue, forget-me-not, lupine and iris.
0.5 Oak Tree Jct. Stay on the road which now climbs more steeply.
0.7 Winter streamlet. Runoff from the north-facing hillside supplies
water for lush growing ferns, mosses and lichens.
0.9 Wildflowers. A colorful, changing wildflower display includes
yellow buttercup, monkeyflower, mule ears, blue dicks, larkspur,
Chinese houses, iris, pink shooting star and clover.
0.9 Boy Scout Jct. Continue uphill on the road. Ahead are views
southwest to the Bolinas-Fairfax Rd. In 1884, it was a stagecoach
road to Bolinas, once Marin's largest town as loggers provided lumber
for San Francisco. Further on, lichen and moss decorate the oaks.
1.3 Five Corners Jct. Turn left onto Yolanda Trail signed to Six Pts
and climb steeply past blue dicks, lupine and iris.
1.4 Junction. The first of four small unmarked junctions before Six
Pts. Keep right in each case. A large madrone surrounded by purple
and creamy iris stand at the hilltop overlooking Hidden Meadow. Good
views south to the water treatment plant and to Mt Tam.
1.7 Madrones. Here is a fine stand of red-trunked madrone trees.
1.8 Junction with Hidden Meadow Trail. Keep left on the road.
1.9 Six Points Jct. Take the first left, Six Pts Trail, down a narrow
path marked by small wooden erosion barriers. Watch for red
columbine and blue larkspur in April.
2.4 Downhill. The trail parallels a small creek rushing downhill
through dense oak-bay woodlands and past small groves of redwood.
2.5 Oak Tree Jct. Turn right and backtrack along Deer Park Rd.
3.0 Parking area with water, tables and restroom facilities.

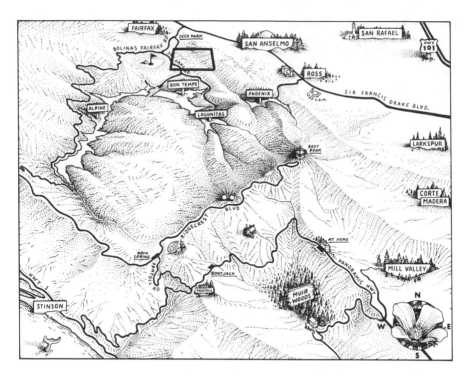

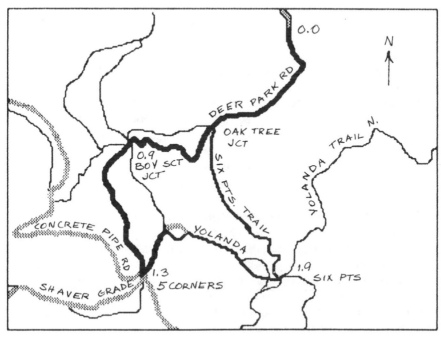

24 Deer Park Rd - Yolanda North

Distance: 3.3 miles
Elevation Change: 400'
Rating: Hiking - 9   Running - 8
When to Go: Good November to May, best February through April.
One of the three best wildflower hikes on Mt Tam. The hike begins
with a steady climb, then skirts a hillside to a viewpoint.

0.0 Start at Deer Park in Fairfax. From the parking area, go left
around the school and through the field. Deer Park Rd begins at the
gate just past a large bay tree and climbs slowly past majestic oaks with
nearby madrone and buckeye trees. Wildflowers along the road
include white milkmaids, slim Solomon, yellow buttercup,
monkeyflower, blue hound's tongue, forget-me-not, lupine and iris.
0.5 Oak Tree Jct. Stay on the road which now climbs more steeply.
0.9 Wildflowers. A colorful, changing spring wildflower display
includes yellow buttercup, mule ears, blue dicks, larkspur, Chinese
houses, iris, pink shooting star and red clarkia.
0.9 Boy Scout Jct. Continue uphill on the road.
1.3 Five Corners Jct. Turn left onto the Yolanda Trail (still a road here)
signed to Six Pts and climb steeply.
1.4 Junction. The first of four small unmarked junctions before Six
Pts. Keep right in each case. On the hilltop, a large madrone
overlooks Hidden Meadow. Great views to Mt Tam.
1.8 Junction with Hidden Meadow Trail. Keep left on the road.
1.9 Six Points Jct. Take the Yolanda Trail, second left, signed
towards Worn Spring. The narrow trail follows the hillside in and out of
wooded stands of oak, bay and madrone.
2.1 Knoll. Take the spur trail left about 100 feet onto an oak-covered
knoll. Lichen and moss cover the tree trunks. Continue back on the
main trail.
2.3 Wildflowers. An open hillside displays more flowers including
white woodland star and yellow cream cups.
2.6 Junction with Worn Spring Rd. Turn left. Good views.
2.9 Junction. Follow the signed Deer Park Trail left as it descends in
switchbacks down the hillside. Lots of wildflowers bloom here in early
spring, followed later by the sweet smelling buckeye tree in May. At
the bottom of the hill, bear right towards the schoolyard.
3.3 Parking area with water, picnic tables and restroom.

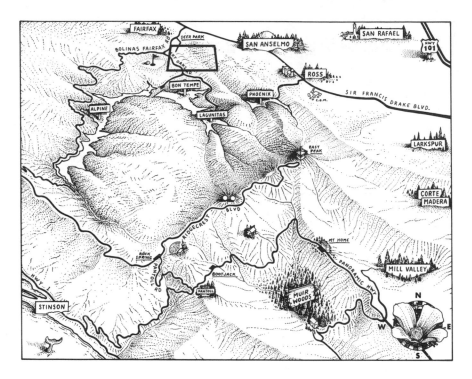

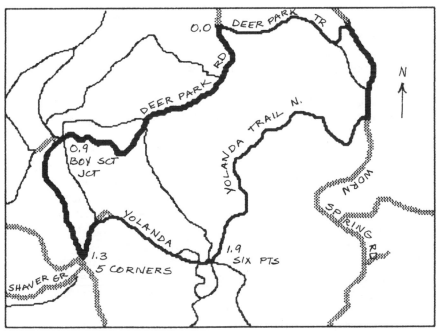

25 Taylor Trail - Bullfrog Rd

Distance: 3.2 miles
Elevation Change: 250'
Rating: Hiking - 6   Running - 9
When to Go: Good November to May, best February to April.
This is a good hike, mostly along roads, through open and wooded
areas with a wide selection of wildflowers and local views.

0.0 Start at the parking area just past the toll booth and walk back
towards the toll booth past large oaks on the right.
0.2 Junction. The Taylor Trail begins next to the Ranger Station and
starts down parallel to the main road. The trail passes by a large
multiple-trunk bay tree, then heads into the first of two stands of
madrones. Early flowers include white milkmaids, woodland star,
yellow buttercup, sun cups, blue hound's tongue and iris.
0.6 Oaks. The trail crosses chert rocks on a hillside with young
madrones starting up under lichen-covered oaks.
0.7 Junction with Concrete Pipe Rd. Bear right. Spring flowers
include white popcorn flower, modesty, blue dicks, Chinese houses,
baby-blue eyes, lupine, larkspur and pink shooting star scattered
along the road. White slim Solomon and pink trillium are at the bend
where the road begins to climb.
1.4 Five Corners Jct. Take the first right to climb steeply up Shaver
Grade. This road is named for Isaac Shaver, a lumberman who ran a
mill near the Alpine Dam site in 1865.
2.0 Views and junction. Good views north just before the junction.
Cross Sky Oaks Rd and take the trail into Douglas fir.
2.1 Junction. Take either the dirt road or the parallel trail down
towards Alpine Lake. Search for yellow poppies along the road and
deer on the hillside. Notice the conifer shores of Alpine Lake.
2.4 Junction to Bon Tempe Dam. Continue right on the road.
2.5 Alpine Lake and picnic spot. Look for two geese that have made
Alpine their home for several years. Good views south to Mt Tam. To
continue the hike, go past the gate along Bullfrog Rd.
2.9 Rock quarry. An old quarry with red-brown sandstone and
blue-green serpentine lies along the road. Golf course ahead.
3.0 Junction. Keep right and explore the moss and lichen growing
on the serpentine rocks peeking through the thin hillside soil.
3.2 Parking area with restroom and water near the Ranger Station.

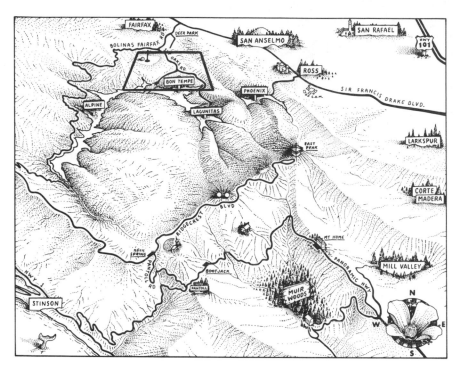

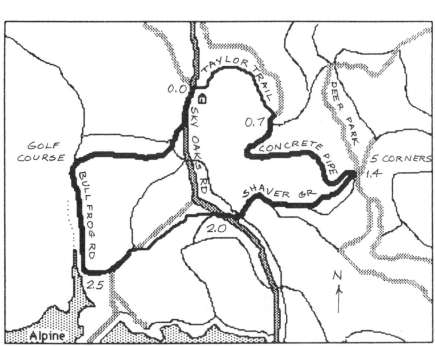

26 Bon Tempe Lake Trail

Distance: 3.9 miles
Elevation Change: 50'
Rating: Hiking - 9   Running - 10
When to Go: Good anytime, best in spring.
This is the best of the three lake hikes. It goes along wooded and open hillsides with many wildflowers and good views.

0.0 From the parking area at Bon Tempe Dam, head up along the dam. Great views to Mt Tam left and to Alpine Lake right. Look for two geese that have made Alpine their home for several years.

0.3 Junction. At dam's end, take the signed Bon Tempe Trail into oak-bay woodland. March flowers include white milkmaids, woodland star, blue hound's tongue and iris.

0.7 Bridge. The first of 3 bridges along the "dark side" of Bon Tempe. Up ahead, many of the taller trees are black oak, too tall to clearly see their distinctive leaves, which are 4-6 inches long with deep lobes. Look for them on the path.

1.0 Bridge. The trail crosses a creek under a canopy of redwood, Douglas fir, oak and bay trees. Lots of shrub-like tanoak underneath.

1.4 Grassland. Yellow gold fields, buttercup, sun cups, blue lupine and pink shooting star inhabit the open area here.

1.8 Junction. Look for trillium under the redwoods. Just past the redwood grove, go left across the bridge. The road skirts the Lagunitas parking area and continues on around the lake.

2.0 Junction. The road heads inland here. Go up 50' and take the trail left. Thirty feet to the right of the junction, notice the large oak and madrone locked in a tight wrestling match.

2.4 Oaks. Large oaks stand majestically on a small peninsula overlooking the lake. Occasionally, osprey and great blue heron are seen here. Cormorants, gulls and wintering ducks are common.

2.9 Junction with Lagunitas Road. Go left. Ahead, the paved ramp provides fishing access for wheelchairs when the lake is full.

3.0 Junction. Leave the road to follow the trail around the "sunny side" of the lake. Watch for yellow sun cups, buttercup, poppy, white popcorn flower, iris and hillsides of blue lupine.

3.7 Junction. Follow the road past the pumphouse and up the hill, then head downhill to join up with the approach road.

3.9 Back at the parking area. Restroom only.

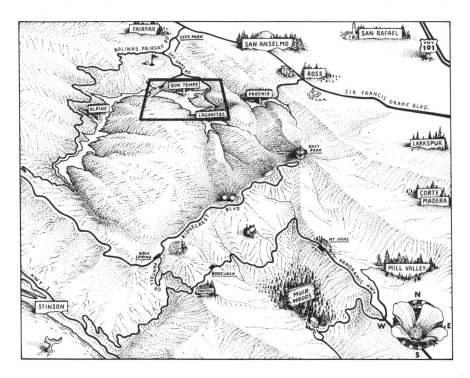

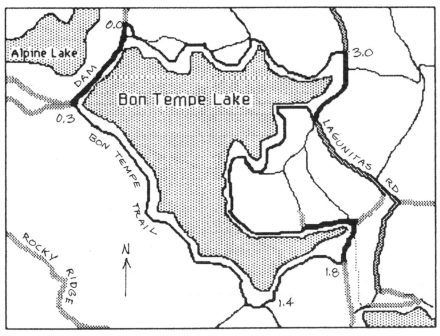

27 Kent Trail - Rocky Ridge Rd

Distance: 5.5 miles
Elevation Change: 500'
Rating: Hiking - 10   Running - 4
When to Go: Good anytime, best in spring.
An exhilarating hike along the conifer shores of Alpine Lake, up through a redwood forest, emerging onto a ridge with good views.

0.0 Start at Bon Tempe Dam. From the parking area, go across the spillway and along the dam. To the right is Alpine Lake. Look for two geese that have made Alpine their home for several years.
0.3 Junction. At dam's end, continue right past lichen-covered oaks. In February, look for white milkmaids, yellow buttercup, pink shooting star, blue hound's tongue and ceanothus among the ferns, mosses and rocks along the road bank. Good views across the lake.
0.8 Kent Trail. Follow the narrow trail as it winds along the lake through a mixture of chaparral and woods with red Indian warrior.
1.9 Views. Great views of conifer forest across the lake like the high Sierra. Just ahead, Van Wyck canyon, a gorgeous canyon of tall redwood, bay, ferns and mosses. Lots of huckleberry.
2.3 Big Fir. A giant Douglas fir stands on a small knoll watching over skinny madrones. A side trunk is as big as the main trunk. Up ahead, enter into a silted canyon with a narrow stream bed.
2.5 Junction. Just opposite the sign, Helen Markt Tr, take the Kent Trail left uphill past exposed waterpipe. This trail was originally called the Swede George Trail after an oldtimer who had a cabin in the area around 1870.
2.8 Canyon and forest. The trail enters a large canyon covered with tall oaks, bay and redwood. Up past a slide, the trail skirts Foul Pool and follows the creek through redwood forest.
3.5 Junction. Take the signed Stocking Trail left. The trail heads downhill skirting Hidden Lake, then uphill along a creek bed.
4.1 Junction with Rocky Ridge Rd. Turn left and go up the road 200' for great views south and east. Continue on the road.
4.9 Junction. At the far edge of a Douglas fir stand reaching up from the lake, look for the Casey Cutoff trailhead to Bon Tempe.
5.2 Oaks and lichen. A large oak, covered with lichen and moss, stands below the serpentine outcropping. Good picnic site.
5.5 Back at the parking area. Restroom facilities only.

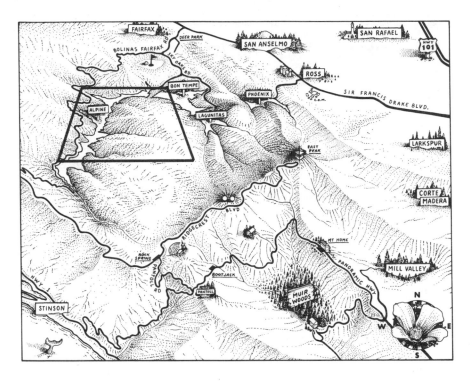

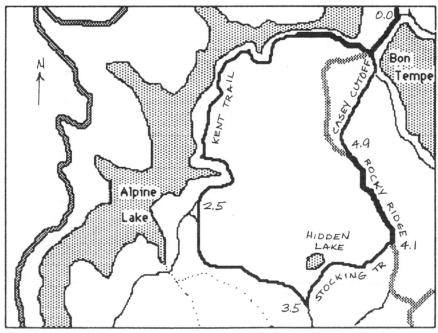

28 Lake Lagunitas Rd

Distance: 1.8 miles
Elevation Change: 50'
Rating: Hiking - 9   Running - 10
When to Go: Good November to May, best February to April.
This is a level hike on roads around the lake with mosses, redwoods, oaks and views of the lake and Mt Tam. Good birding area.

0.0 Start at the Lagunitas parking lot. If you're fortunate, you might hear or see the pileated woodpecker nearby. It is a large 15" woodpecker with a black body, partially white neck and red tufted head. To start the hike, go into the picnic area and pick up the trail next to the spillway. Climb up to the dam. There are many other birds around the lake, including wintering water birds and, occasionally, an osprey flying over the treetops.
0.2 Dam. Go right over the spillway, to circle the lake counterclockwise. See if you can spot the rare Pacific Pond turtles sunning on the floating logs by the dam. In February, watch for white milkmaids, red Indian warrior and blue hound's tongue under a mixed forest of oak, bay, madrone and redwood trees.
0.3 Junction with Rock Spring - Lagunitas Road. Continue left.
0.5 Bridge. The first of 3 bridges crosses a creek supporting redwoods. You rarely see moss on redwoods, but often can find a grey-green lichen on the trunk. Tanoak is the dominant shrub here. Look for red Indian paintbrush and iris as well as huckleberry ahead.
0.7 Bridge and Junction to Colier Spring. Continue left.
0.9 Mosses. In winter, a fine display of mosses, lichens, ferns, succulents and other moisture lovers grows along the rocky hillside. Look for pink shooting star and hazel with its fuzzy leaves.
1.2 Bridge. Under a canopy of tall oaks and madrones, the road crosses the East Fork of Lagunitas Creek. Great lichens on the oaks. Bear left at the bridge and again at Lakeview Rd. Across the road are non-native Coulter pines with the heaviest cones of all pines.
1.4 Junction. The road uphill leads to the Pilot Knob Trail. Continue left past the large moss-covered oak at the junction.
1.5 Junction. The road veers right up to the ranger's residence. Stay left on the trail as it passes through French broom and down the stairs to the dam. At the dam, turn right to go down the road.
1.8 Parking area. Water, picnic tables and restroom facilities.

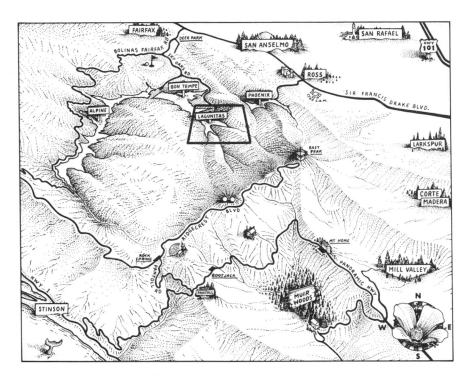

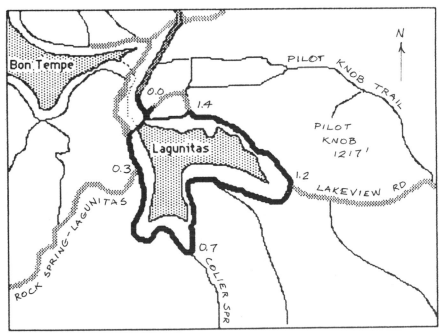

29 Lakeview Rd to Pilot Knob

Distance: 2.2 miles
Elevation Change: 500'
Rating: Hiking - 8   Running - 9
When to Go: Good November to May, best February to April.
This is a good hike through mixed forest, climbing to Pilot Knob for great views, then passing the largest Madrone seen anywhere.

0.0 Start at the Lagunitas parking lot. Take the road overlooking the picnic area up to the dam. February flowers include white milkmaids and blue hound's tongue under the oak, bay and madrone trees.
0.2 Dam. Look for the rare and endangered Pacific Pond Turtles that often sun themselves on the floating logs by the dam. Go left up the stairs past the ranger residence and on to Lakeview Road.
0.3 Trees. The road passes by large madrones with smooth red bark and tall oaks clothed with grey-green lichen.
0.5 Coulter Pines. These pines are identified by their long needles and heavy cones. Look for yellow buttercup, poppy, sun cups and iris in early spring and the yellow mariposa lily in May and June.
0.6 Junction. The road right goes around the lake. Stay left. Views to Mt Tam on the right and Pilot Knob on the left.
1.1 Junction. Take the signed trail to Pilot Knob left up the hill. The trail climbs steeply through tall madrone, oak, and conifer trees with lower growing tanoak and huckleberry. Early flowers include yellow sanicle, white zigadene and iris.
1.4 Junction. At a knoll, next to a large bay tree, take the spur trail left uphill to Pilot Knob. Ahead, notice the grove of young redwoods that will someday overgrow the tall madrone nearby.
1.5 Pilot Knob 1217'. Great views south to Mt Tam, west to Bon Tempe Lake and to Mt Diablo in the east bay. To continue the hike, return down the spur trail and bear left along the main trail.
1.8 Madrone. The grandfather of madrones! An incredible madrone tree with six main trunks, each the size of a single madrone. The tree has limited foliage and may not last many more years. The trail continues along the ridgetop past lichen-covered oaks and more normal-sized madrone trees.
2.1 Junction. The road left returns along the lake. Head right past redwood, Douglas fir, oak and madrone trees to the parking lot.
2.2 Parking lot. Water, tables, barbecue, map and restrooms.

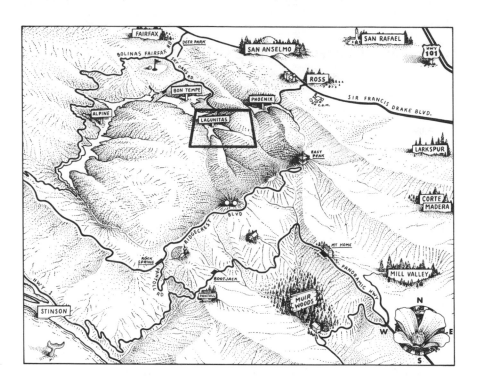

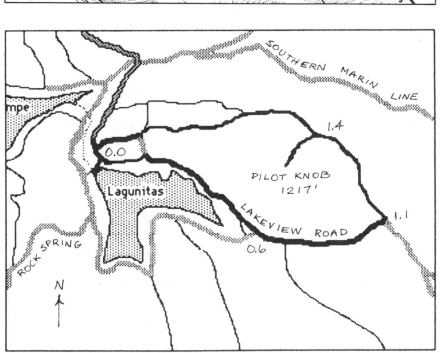

30 Madrone - Pumpkin Ridge Trails

Distance: 3.6 miles
Elevation Change: 700' of ups and downs
Rating: Hiking - 8   Running - 6
When to Go: Good November to May, best in March and April.
This hike explores the rolling hills south of Bon Tempe Lake. Good views and good wildflowers are along the open and wooded ridges.

0.0 Start at the Lagunitas parking lot and head west to the edge of Bon Tempe Lake. Follow the dirt road past the large valves out to Sky Oaks Rd. Watch for yellow sun cups, buttercup, blue lupine and a pale purple lily, calochortus, along the open road.
0.3 Junction with Sky Oaks Rd. Go right down the paved road past two storage areas. Look for red paintbrush, white modesty, woodland star, milkmaids, blue hound's tongue and larkspur.
0.5 Two junctions. Take the dirt road, Fish Gulch, left towards Phoenix Lake, then leave the road and take the Fish Gulch Trail left steeply downhill past yellow monkeyflower and blue dicks.
1.0 Junction. Just past the small building, take the signed Madrone Trail uphill. Majestic madrone and oak trees beckon ahead.
1.5 Unmarked Junction. A Douglas fir stands at the junction of two trails, take the Pumpkin Ridge Trail right.
1.8 Junction with Sky Oaks Rd. Cross the road and climb the washed out trail up the open hillside. On the hilltop, there are great views and lots of lupine, buttercup and white popcorn flower. Follow the small road over two more hills before heading downhill. Halfway downhill, the road abruptly ends and a trail continues straight, then veers left towards a power line.
2.2 Junction. About 150' before the dirt road to Alpine Lake, take the trail left up towards a saddle between two tree-covered hilltops. Notice the non-native Coulter pines with large cones.
2.5 Junction. Head left along the lake past yellow poppies.
2.8 Junction with Sky Oaks Rd. Head right, past the restroom, then climb uphill 50' to the trail, and bear right again.
3.1 Junction with Sky Oaks Rd. Cross the road again and take the dirt road uphill about 200', then take the trail left downhill. Ahead, madrones and Douglas fir battle for sunlight.
3.5 Junction with lake. Go past the valves to the parking area.
3.6 Parking area with water, tables, barbecue and restrooms.

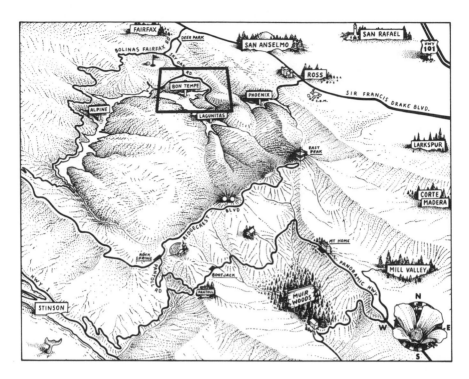

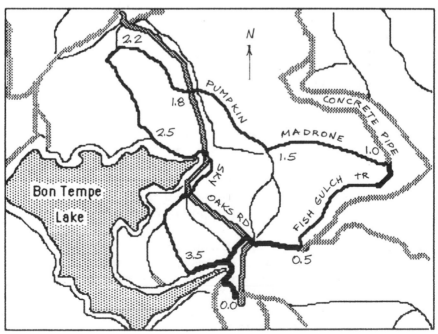

31 Colier Spring - North Side Trails

Distance: 4.6 miles
Elevation Change: 1200'
Rating: Hiking - 9   Running - 2
When to Go: Good anytime, best in spring.
A good mountain climb along a cascading creek, then an easy
descent through an interesting mixture of flora; good views north.

0.0 Start at the Lagunitas parking lot. Go into the picnic area and pick
up the trail next to the spillway. Climb past redwoods to the dam and
head right, counterclockwise around the lake. Early flowers include
white milkmaids, red Indian warrior and blue hound's tongue under a
forest of oak, bay, madrone and redwood.
0.7 Bridge and Junction to Colier Spring. Turn right and follow the
trail up the left side of the creek through the redwood forest.
0.8 Creek crossing. Continue up the right side of the creek.
1.0 Creek crossing. Cross over to the left side of the creek.
1.2 Creek junction and crossing. Two creeks come tumbling
together here. Upstream, cross this creek and follow the steep trail up
and over to the next ridgetop paralleling the west creek.
1.4 Last crossing. Cross the creek near a large madrone and big leaf
maple and climb steeply past moss-covered boulders.
1.8 Colier Spring at 1925' and a bench for resting. The spring was
named after John Monroe Colier, a wealthy but eccentric Scotsman
who worked on various trails in the late 1800's. Notice the unusual
chain fern with deeply cut blades. To continue the hike, take the first
trail on the right, signed, Lower North Side Tr. This trail moves gently
downhill, passing through an interesting mixture of forest and
chaparral. Chaparral includes toyon, manzanita, ceanothus, chamise
and chaparral oak. Good views north. Up ahead, coffeeberry, iris,
chain fern, white zigadene, calochortus, oak, Douglas fir, madrone,
moss-covered rocks, wood rose and nutmeg create a native plant
exhibition.
2.7 Junction. Just past the serpentine rocks, take the signed road
right towards Lake Lagunitas. Continue right at the next two road
junctions. Spring flowers among the chaparral include monkeyflower,
false lupine, yerba santa and chaparral pea.
4.3 Junction with Lake Lagunitas. Bear left towards the dam.
4.6 Parking area. Water, picnic tables and restroom facilities.

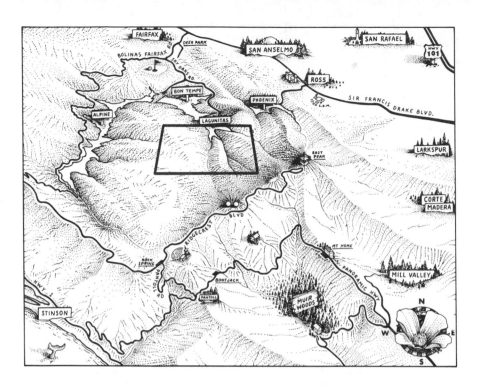

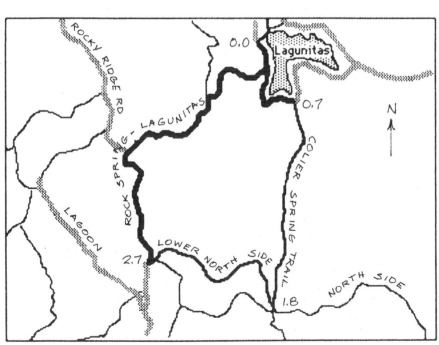

32 Cataract - High Marsh Trails

Distance: 7.7 miles
Elevation Change: 1100', 300' and 700'
Rating: Hiking - 10   Running - 4
When to Go: Good anytime, best February to May.
A strenuous but spectacular hike in the most remote section of the mountain. Wonderful pools, waterfalls and conifer forests.

0.0 Park anywhere south of Alpine Dam and walk to the signed trailhead 0.2 miles from the Dam. The trail starts along the lake in a conifer forest with some bay, oak and big leaf maple. Early shade tolerant wildflowers include white modesty, milkmaids, pink wood rose, trillium, blue hound's tongue, mission bells and iris.
0.1 Two junctions. At the first junction, bear right, but stay along the lake. Ahead, cross the creek and continue by the lake.
0.3 Cataract Creek. The trail begins a steep climb up the right side of the creek past refreshing views of pools and waterfalls.
0.7 Bridge and junction. Above the bridge, bear right past a spectacular creekside setting. Ahead, the trail levels somewhat.
1.0 Sunlight. A small open hillside lets in light to grow yellow buttercup and baby blue-eyes. Up ahead, scenery typical of Hawaii.
1.4 Junction with High Marsh Trail. Continue right.
1.5 Laurel Dell picnic area. Water, tables, restroom and meadow. Backtrack down the trail and take High Marsh Trail right. On the open hillside, look for white woodland star, popcorn flower, yellow fiddleneck, poppy and blue dicks. Continue left along the main trail at each junction ahead.
3.4 Bridge. Just past the Kent Trail junction, cross the bridge and continue straight uphill past side trails.
3.6 Junction at Serpentine Knoll. Bear left and head downhill.
4.0 Junction. Take the signed Kent Trail left towards Alpine Lake. The trail descends through an enchanting redwood and tanoak forest, then past a large slide on Swede George Creek.
5.0 Junction with Alpine Lake. Go left as the trail soon leaves the lake and traverses the ridges. Ahead, the trail crosses Swede George Creek on a bridge built from lumber floated across the lake.
7.0 Junction and bridge. After a long climb, bear right to retrace your steps alongside Cataract Creek.
7.7 Back at the trailhead. No facilities.

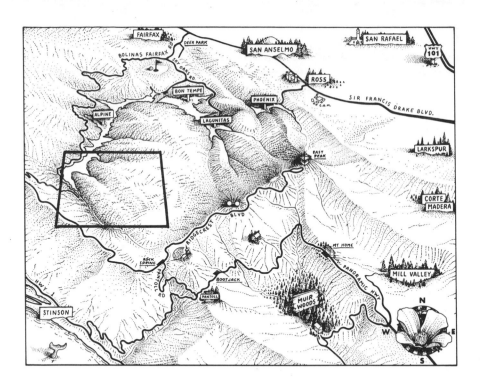

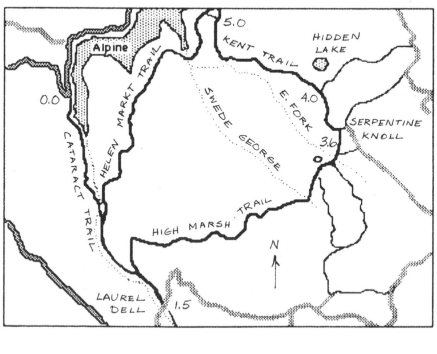

A1 Combination Hikes

The 32 hikes in this book were created to be "modular", so that it would be easy to combine two or more hikes into hikes of longer distance. Here are just a few possible combinations:

C1 Distance: 8.7 miles   Elevation Change: 1400'
This hike starts at the Mt Home and explores both sides of the mountain passing by West Point Inn, Mt Theater and Rock Spring.
0.0 Start at the Mt Home and follow Hike 7 from mile 0.0 to 1.9
1.9 From West Point Inn, follow Hike 15 from mile 3.1 to 4.9
3.7 From Rock Spring, continue on Hike 15 from mile 0.0 to 3.1
6.8 From West Point Inn, take Hike 7 backwards from mile 1.9 to 0.0
8.7 Back at Mt Home.

C2 Distance: 9.4 miles   Elevation Change: 1700'
This hike starts at Mt Home and follows the south side of the mountain all the way to Steep Ravine and back.
0.0 Start at the Mt Home and follow Hike 6 from mile 0.0 to 1.9
1.9 From Alpine Jct, follow Hike 8 backwards from mile 3.4 to 3.0
2.3 From Pantoll, follow Hike 11 from mile 0.0 to 2.0
4.3 From Steep Ravine, follow Hike 11 from mile 2.0 to 3.6
5.9 From Pantoll, follow Hike 8 from mile 3.0 to 3.4
6.3 From Alpine Jct, follow Hike 6 from mile 1.9 to 5.0
9.4 Back at Mt Home.

C3 Distance: 5.4 miles   Elevation Change: 800'
This hike circles Phoenix Lake, then climbs Shaver Grade to return via the Yolanda Trail.
0.0 Start at Phoenix Lake and take Hike 18 from mile 0.0 to 1.6
1.6 From Phoenix Jct, follow Hike 21 from mile 1.0 to 2.7
3.3 From Six Points Jct, continue on Hike 21 from mile 2.7 to 4.8
5.4 Back at Phoenix Lake parking.

C4 Distance: 8.9 miles   Elevation Change: 1700'
This hike starts at Lake Lagunitas and climbs to the East Peak.
0.0 Start at Lagunitas Lake and take Hike 31 from mile 0.0 to 1.8
1.8 From Colier Spring, follow Hike 17 from mile 3.1 to 4.2
2.9 From East Peak, continue on Hike 17 from mile 0.0 to 3.1
6.0 From Colier Spring, take Hike 31 from mile 1.8 to 4.6
8.8 Back at Lagunitas Lake parking lot.

A2 A Selection Of Best Trails

Not sure where to go? Here is our selection of best trails to guide you. Remember that the season and weather influence trail conditions.

The 3 Best Creeks and Waterfall Trails
1. Steep Ravine, Hike 11
2. Cataract Creek, Hike 32 is best, but also Hikes 12, 13, 14
3. Redwood Creek, Hike 4

The 3 Best Wildflower Trails
1. Yolanda Trail, both north and south, Hikes 21 and 24
2. Coastal Trail, Hike 12
3. Sun Trail, Hike 3

The 3 Best View Trails
1. Verna Dunshee Trail, Hike 16
2. Old Mine Trail, Hikes 10 and 12
3. A three way tossup between the Coastal Trail, Hike 12, Northside Trail, Hikes 15 and 31, and Bald Hill, Hike 20

The 3 Best Running Trails
1. All three lake trails are good, Hikes 18, 26 and 28
2. TCC Trail, Hike 8
3. Troop 80 Trail, Hike 6

The 3 Best Birding Trails
1. Lake Lagunitas Road, Hike 28
2. Simmons Trail, Hike 13
3. Bon Tempe Lake Trail, Hike 26

The 3 Best Flora Trails
1. Steep Ravine, Hike 12
2. Northside Trail, Hikes 15 and 31
3. Simmons Trail, Hike 13

The 3 Best Beginners Trails
1. Bon Tempe Lake Trail, Hike 26
2. Muir Woods - Fern Creek, Hike 2
3. Potrero Meadows - Laurel Dell, Hike 14

A3 What Others Say

We asked several veteran Mt Tam people, "What is your favorite hike?"
Here is their response:

Wilma Follette
Botanist and hike leader for the California Native Plant Society
  "I like the Benstein, Mickey O'Brien and Cataract Trails
  (Hikes 13 and 14) for spring wildflowers and rare plants."

Jim Furman
President of the Tamalpa Runners
  "The Matt Davis Extension (Hike 12) and the Old Mine
  Trail (Hike 10) offer great views."

Dave Gould
Mt Tamalpais State Park Ranger and Executive Secretary for
the Mt Tamalpais Interpretative Association
  "The Coastal Trail (Hike 12) for the spectacular views
  and wildflowers."

Casey May
Chief Ranger for Marin Municipal Water District
  "I like the North Side Trail (Hike 17 and 31) for the
  panoramic views and varied flora."

Bob Stewart
Hike leader and Naturalist for Marin County Parks
  "I enjoy the Sun Trail (Hike 3) in early February
  to see the first wildflowers."

Meryl Sundove
Hike leader and Naturalist for Marin Audubon Society
  "The Lake Lagunitas area (Hike 28) is one of the best
  places to see local and migrating birds."

Mia Monroe Way
Hike leader and Muir Woods Ranger
  "My favorite hike is to go down the Panoramic and
  Lost trails into Fern Canyon (Hike 5)."

A4 A Trail For All Seasons

December - January
The sun is at its lowest angle of the year and it's often cold and wet. Rainfall averages 20 inches during these two months. But you can beat the indoor blues by getting out and looking for views, creeks, waterfalls, mosses and lichens, or southern exposures. Hikes 6, 7, 9, 10, 13, 14, 20 and 22 are good choices.

February - March
This is the premier hiking time of the year. Even though rainfall averages 16 inches, the weather is getting better, and water runoff is high. Trillium, milkmaids and hound's tongue start the wildflower parade. All the hikes are at their best, especially Hikes 2, 3, 6, 11, 13, 14, 21, 22, 23, 24, 28, 31, and 32.

April - May
More great hiking time. The weather is at its best, the hills are green and the late wildflowers reach their peak. All the hikes are great, especially Hikes 4, 5, 11, 12, 13, 14, 15, 17, 22, 27, 30, 31, and 32.

June - July
While most of the mountain is hot and dry, Muir Woods and Steep Ravine are often cool and foggy as the Bay Area air-conditioning system runs full blast. Some summer wildflowers, mariposa lily, monkeyflower, poppy, yarrow and clarkia hang on while the hills turn brown. Hikes 1, 2, and 11.

August - September
Now is the time to avoid the dry, dusty roads. Head for the north-facing trails, creeks, conifer forests and ripe huckleberries. Hikes 1, 2, 7, 8, 11 and 27.

October - November
Look for fall red colors from poison oak, and yellow and brown colors from big leaf maple and deciduous oaks. First winter storms. Rainfall averages 8 inches during this period settling the dust and bringing forth mushrooms. Great weather with gusty winds, clear days and marvelous views. It's a good time to head for the south-facing trails and the oak - bay woodlands around the lakes. Hikes 7, 9, 10, 11, 16, 17, 18, 26, 28, 29 and 30.

A5 Geology of Mt Tamalpais

In The Beginning

Several billion years ago, dozens of giant stars formed in our section of the Milky Way Galaxy, lived a short intense life, then died in a cataclysmic explosion called a "supernova". During that explosion, most of the elements heavier than hydrogen and helium were created and spewed forth into the galaxy to be collected and used by later generations of stars, including our sun.

In our solar system, these heavier elements, carbon, oxygen, iron, radioactive uranium, etc, are most noticeable on the inner planets, especially earth. During it's early stages, the earth started out with a cool interior and hot surface caused by meteor bombardment. Later, the surface cooled, but the interior heated up due to the slow release of radioactivity by the heaviest of the supernova elements. Today, the earth has a thin crustal surface of rocks floating on a hot molten interior.

Plate Tectonics

The theory of plate tectonics suggests that the earth's surface, the upper 40 miles, is composed of six major rigid plates that move on a plastic interior created by the hot radioactive elements. These plates are constantly interacting as new plate material oozes up in some areas, like Iceland, and old plate material disappears in other areas, like the Aleutians.

The Pacific plate, containing Point Reyes, Los Angeles and most of the Pacific Ocean, is moving northwest relative to the North American plate and is slowly disappearing into the Alaskan trench. Although the Pacific plate is moving at an average speed of 2" per year, the motion is not steady. For example, where the two plates meet, as they do along the San Andreas and related fault lines, there can be sudden plate motions of up to 20 feet as happened in the big San Francisco quake of 1906.

Mt Tamalpais Rocks

Surprisingly, most of Mt Tamalpais is not the result of collisions between the Pacific plate and the North American plate. Geologists believe that Mt Tamalpais was created when the North American plate overrode a pre-Pacific plate between 20 and 60 million years ago. This pre-Pacific plate now lies under the western United States where in the pummelling process of getting there, it produced mountains, volcanoes, hot springs, geysers, and a variety of rock and mineral formations, largely remnants of the old sea floor. The rocks on Mt Tamalpais, along with most of the Bay Area peninsula and mountain rocks, have been named the Franciscan group, after San Francisco.

The most noticible rocks of the Franciscan group on Mt Tamalpais are sandstones, shale, chert and serpentine.

Sandstone and Shale

Sandstone and shale are sedimentary rocks formed by the erosion and deposit of small particles carried out to sea. Often, plate tectonics will lift sandstone deposits up to form hills and mountains. Sandstone is usually grey, tan or yellow in color depending on the mineral content.

Chert

Chert is a shiny brittle quartz rock formed from the skeletal remains of animals raining onto the seafloor where eventually they are heated and crystalized in the presense of a rock called greenstone. Although not common, chert is quite noticeable due to its strong reddish, brown or white coloring and due to its sharp hard surface that clicks when walked on, sounding like porcelain rubbed together. On Mt Tamalpais, chert outcroppings can be seen and heard at the bottom of the Taylor Trail, Hike 25.

Serpentine

Serpentine rocks are formed by combining water with the mantel rock, peridotite. Serpentine is usually grey or grey-green in color and some forms have a smooth soapy feel. Serpentine outcroppings are quite noticeable on both sides of the mountain ridgeline, especially along the Rock Spring, Simmons, North Side and Old Mine trails (Hikes 9, 10, 13, 14, 15). Serpentine samples can also be seen in front of the Pantoll Ranger Station.

Serpentine Flora

Botanists like serpentine because it produces unusual plant life. Serpentine soil is high in magnesium and low in calcium, nitrogen and phosphorous. Some species of flora, like redwoods, avoid serpentine completely. Other flora, like Sargent cypress and certain species of oak, manzanita and ceanothus only grow on serpentine soils. In general, serpentine soil produces sparse growth or reduced growth and in extreme cases, no flora at all.

A6 Climate of Mt Tamalpais

Overview

The earth revolves slowly on its north-south axis like a giant roast in a cosmic barbecue. The sun provides the heat, but the sun heats the earth unevenly with the equatorial regions receiving more energy than the poles. It is this difference in heating coupled with the difference in absorption and release of energy by the atmosphere, oceans and land mass that drives the earth's weather system.

One of the dominant rhythms in this weather system is the jet stream that circles the northern latitudes like a high flying roller coaster. In winter, when the jet stream dips down over northern California, it often delivers a series of low pressure storm systems to Mt Tamalpais and brings life-giving rain.

Mt Tamalpais

The climate on Mt Tamalpais consists of warm dry summers and mild wet winters characteristic of the Mediterranean region in Europe. In winter, most of Mt Tamalpais has a uniform climate. Rainfall ranges from 42" per year at Pantoll to 52" per year at Lake Lagunitas. January temperatures average from 44-46 degrees Fahrenheit while the top of Mt Tamalpais is a little colder and the coastal areas are a little milder. While winter climates are fairly uniform, summer climates offer more variation and create different climate zones. For this book, we have identified five climate zones.

Zone A - Summer Fogbelt

This climate zone is dominated by the Pacific Ocean and its summertime fog. The zone lies along the coast and up into Frank's Valley and Muir Woods to about 1500'. Exposed areas are often grassland, while ravines are wooded. Large ravines, created by heavy water runoff, like Steep Ravine and Muir Woods are ideal places for redwoods. These ravines are good places to visit in hot summer weather.

Zone B - Summer Windbelt

This climate zone occurs on exposed peaks, ridges, knolls and hills, such as Bolinas Ridge, East Peak and Bald Hill. The conditions that create the summer fogbelt also produce this climate zone. The California central valley gets hot and the hot air rises, drawing in cool ocean air.

Strong westerly winds of 25-40 miles per hour roar across these exposed areas almost every afternoon. Because winter erosion of peaks leaves thin soil, usually this zone only supports annual grasses or wind-pruned chaparral.

Zone C - Steep South-Facing Slopes

This climate zone occurs along the steep south-facing slopes of Mt Tamalpais, Bald Hill and other tall hills around the lakes. Summer and winter daytime temperatures are higher here than in surrounding areas. Steep slopes and thin soil usually produce chaparral or grasslands. Wildflowers show up first here, for example, on the Sun and Yolanda Trails. These areas are good places to visit in winter and early spring.

Zone D - Steep North-Facing Slopes

This zone lies along the the steep north-facing slopes below the three peaks of Mt Tamalpais, and also on Pilot Knob and Bald Hill. Winter sun is almost nonexistent and at the higher elevation, summers are cooler. Vegetation is usually more dense here as can be seen on the East Peak Loop. The difference between Zone C and Zone D vegetation can also clearly be seen on Bald Hill and Pilot Knob. Wildflowers usually bloom 4-6 weeks later here than in Zone C.

Zone E - Plateau Areas.

This zone occurs around the lakes and in the Rock Spring Area. At lower elevations around the lakes, eroded soil has accumulated and supports more tree growth, usually the oak - bay hardwood community. Wildflowers begin in February and March, 2-4 weeks after Zone C.

A7 History of Mt Tamalpais

The First People
The last ice age ended about 12,000 years ago, but when it reached its peak, the Pacific Ocean was almost 400 feet lower than it is today. San Francisco Bay did not exist then and Mt Tamalpais was 30 miles from the coast. If California natives lived along the Pacific coast or along the great river that flowed past what is now the Golden Gate, the settlements have long been inundated.

It is not known when the first people arrived in the Bay Area. Those who later settled in Marin are known as the Coastal Miwok Indians. The oldest known Miwok settlement dates back over 7000 years. There is no record of Indian settlements on Mt Tamalpais itself; it may have been considered sacred. The legend of "The Sleeping Maiden" tells how a young Miwok girl was saved from the devil Diablo tribe by a shuddering of the mountain. Later, her profile could be seen on the mountaintop from a great distance.   There are many versions of the legend and most, if not all, of them were created by 19th and 20th century writers.

Wildlife in early Marin and on Mt Tamalpais was much more abundant than it is today. Migrating birds, tule elk, deer, mountian lions and even grizzly bears roamed the land.

The First Europeans
In June of 1579, Francis Drake landed along the Marin coast. Although Drake's party met the Miwoks and might have seen the mountain, what they recorded were "nipping colds as we have never felt before" and "thick mists and most stinking fog." The first recorded name given to the mountain appeared in 1772 where it was referred to as La Sierra de Nuestro Padre de San Francisco. The present name first appeared as, Tamal pais, around 1845. The name appears to come from two similar sounding Miwok words that mean "coast mountain."

It is not certain who was the first European climber; some evidence points to the Englishman Beechey, in 1826. By the 1870's many people climbed the mountain as described in the April, 1873 edition of the San Francisco Illustrated Press. "The mountain itself is rugged and rough, but the view from the summit will well repay the toil necessary to get there. Small parties occasionally visit the mountain during the summer months when everything is green, but the character of the trail is such that the majority of them are satisfied with the view from half way up." By the 1890's, the mountain became popular enough for Sidney B. Cushing and others to begin planning for a better way to get to the top.

The First Railroad

On August 26, 1896, seventy-five newspapermen took the ferry from San Francisco to Sausalito, then went by electric train to Mill Valley, to board the Mill Valley and Mt Tamalpais Scenic Railway train for a spectacular ride to the top of Mt Tamalpais.

For years, small rugged steam and electric engines carried tourists and travelers up to the famous Double Bow Knot on Mesa Jct at 1000'. From there, the traveler could continue up to the Tavern of Tamalpais near the summit, or take the Gravity car down into Muir Woods. At West Point Inn, the passenger could get off the train and hike to the Mt Theater or take the stage coach to Bolinas.

In its heyday, an estimated 50,000 visitors a year rode to the top of Mt Tamalpais, many of them enjoying the scenery by hiking back down to Mill Valley. By 1925, the increasingly pervasive influence of the automobile produced talk of converting the railroad bed to a toll road. And in 1929, a serious mountain fire dealt the railroad a blow from which it never fully recovered.

Muir Woods National Monument

The redwoods of Muir Woods have been visited by more people than any other redwood grove in the world. Over 1.3 million people annually discover the grandeur and beauty of these magnificient trees.

That this grove of virgin redwoods is still standing today is largely the result of perservance by one man, William Kent. Around 1900, improved logging methods made it feasible to log what was called Sequoia Canyon. Conservationists persuaded Kent to buy and protect the woods. However, the trees were still not safe. In 1907, a local water company condemned the canyon for use as a reservoir. Kent offered to give the land to the Federal Government, but was refused. Then, he tried to persuade Congress to declare the woods a national park, but they rejected the idea. Finally, President Theodore Roosevelt, using his presidential powers, accepted the land as a National Monument in 1908.

Today, Muir Woods is open for day use from 8 AM to sunset. Because of the large number of visitors, camping, picnicking, bicycles and pets are not allowed in the park. There is a small snack and gift shop near the park entrance. For more information, check at the Ranger Station.

Mount Tamalpais State Park

In 1925, developers began advertising lots for sale on the southern slopes of Mt Tamalpais. Alarmed, the Tamalpais Conservation Club, or TCC, began a campaign to preserve the mountain for public use. The TCC was founded in 1912 and became known as the "Guardian of the Mountain". By 1928 the campaign raised over $30,000 to purchase land and to donate it to the State of California. Later, William Kent, a few hours before his death in 1928, gave another 350 acres to the state that included Steep Ravine and the Mountain Theater. The state park was officially created in 1931.

Today, the park occupies over 6000 acres, mostly on the south side, west side and on the ridgeline of the mountain. The two major visiting areas are East Peak and the Mountain Theater. The theater, long an attraction, held its first play back in 1913. Then, the audience sat and the actors performed on the sloping grassy hillside of a natural amphitheater. The current theater, built of 40,000 stones, some up to 4000 pounds, was constructed by the Civilian Conservation Corps, or CCC, in the middle 1930's. Over 200 men worked on the theater and on expanding and improving nearby trails. The theater was carefully constructed as a replica of a Greek amphitheater and named for Sidney B. Cushing, one of the founders of the railroad.

Although East Peak and the Mountain Theater are focal points of the park, the hiking trails, views and flora are the main attractions. Over 30 miles of State Park trails connect with GGNRA, Muir Woods and the Water District trails to create a 200 mile hiking wonderland.

Day use of the park begins 1/2 hour before sunrise and ends 1/2 hour after sunset at the gates across Ridgecrest Boulevard. Picnic areas are located at Bootjack, Pantoll and East Peak, but because of extreme summer fire hazards, the East Peak area does not permit fires or stoves. Limited camping is available near the Ranger Station at Pantoll and a small visitor center is open summer weekends at East Peak. Pets are not allowed on park trails or roads.

For more information about the park or trail information, check at the Ranger Station at Pantoll.

Marin Municipal Water District

The three basic necessities of life are air, water and energy. So it is no surprise to discover that in early times, over 25 enterprising companies used Mt Tamalpais to collect, store and sell water. Today, there is one water company, the Marin Municipal Water District or MMWD. The MMWD was chartered as a public company in 1912. Since that time, it has bought out all the private companies operating on Mt Tamalpais and now owns about 60% of the area shown on the Mt Tamalpais map. Four of the district's seven reservoirs and their watersheds are located on the immediate north side of the mountain. These are:

Reservoir	Year	Dam Height	Area	Rainfall
Lagunitas	1873	50 feet	23 acres	52 inches
Phoenix	1905	95 feet	25 acres	47 inches
Alpine	1918	140 feet	219 acres	49 inches
Bon Tempe	1948	94 feet	130 acres	43 inches

Rainfall records for Lake Lagunitas go back over 100 years and during that period, the heaviest rainfall season was in 1889/90 when over 112 inches of rain was recorded. The minimum rainfall season occurred in 1923/24 when only 19 inches was recorded. The heaviest monthly rainfall occured in January 1896 when 44 inches fell.

The Water District welcomes public use of the watershed with a land policy of "passive use and minimum impact." This policy lets nature take care of the land and vegetation, although fire control, pigs, deer, roads and humans have created some disturbances.

The watershed lands open at 7:00 AM in summer and 8:00 AM in winter until sunset. Hikers, bikers, horses and runners should stay on designated trails and roads. Pets should stay on a leash and fires should be kept in official barbecue pits. Fishing is encouraged and requires possession of a California State fishing license. Swimming in the lakes is prohibited.

The Water District operates one Ranger Station on the mountain, located along the Sky Oaks Road outside of Fairfax. Next to the Ranger Station is the toll booth where a daily fee is collected for bringing a car into the lakes area. For more information about the Water District or current trail conditions, check at the Ranger Station.

A8 White - Cream Wildflowers

Calochortus or Oakland Star Tulip
Calochortus umbellatus
Flower size: 1/2-1 inch
Plant height: 3-10 inches
Leaf length: 1 basal leaf 6-14 inches
Season: March - May
Habitat: Grassy and brushy hills
Location: Hikes 6, 8, 9, 14, 15, 17, 31

Milkmaids
Cardamine californica
Flower size: 1/2 inch
Plant height: 16 inches
Leaf length: 2 inches
Season: January - March
Habitat: Meadows, fields
Location: Widespread

Modesty
Whipplea modesta
Flower size: 1/8 inches
Plant height: 6-12 inches
Leaf length: 1/2-1 inch
Season: March - May
Habitat: Wooded or brushy slopes
Location: Hikes 7, 16, 17, 19, 20, 22, 25, 30, 32

Other common white - cream wildflowers are

Fairy Bells ..... Feb-July, 2 feet, greenish white, bell-shaped flowers
Morning Glory ..... Mar-Sept, 2 feet, twining vine, pinkish white flowers
Pitcher Sage ..... Mar-June, 30 inches tall, bell-shaped white flowers
Yarrow ..... Apr-Sept, 18 inches, fern-like leaves, white flower cluster

Popcorn Flower
Plagiobothrys nothofulvus
Flower size: 1/4 inch
Plant height: 8-16 inches
Leaf length: 1-4 inches
Season: April - May
Habitat: Open grassy slopes and flats
Location: Hikes 12, 14, 20, 21, 26, 30, 32

Slim Solomon
Smilacina stellata var. *sessilifolia*
Flower size: 1/4 inch
Plant height: 1-2 feet
Leaf length: 2-6 inches
Season: February - April
Habitat: Wooded or brushy hills
Location: Hikes 3, 4, 6, 7, 11, 12, 19, 20, 23, 24, 25

Woodland Star
Lithophragma affine
Flower size: 3/4 inches
Plant height: 8-24 inches
Leaf length: 1/2-1 1/2 inches
Season: March - May
Habitat: Shaded and woody slopes
Location: Hikes 19, 20, 23, 24, 25, 26, 28, 30, 32

Zigadene
Zigadenus fremontii
Flower size: 1/2 inch
Plant height: 1-2 feet
Leaf length: 8-24 inches
Season: February - April
Habitat: Wooded or brushy slopes
Location: Widespread, common

A9 Yellow Wildflowers

Buttercup
Ranunculus californicus
Flower size: 1 inch
Plant height: 8-16 inches
Leaf length: 1-1 1/2 inches
Season: February - May
Habitat: Low moist fields and brushy hills
Location: Widespread, common

California Poppy
Eschscholzia californica
Flower size: 1-2 inches
Plant height: 8-16 inches
Leaf length: 1-2 inches
Season: March - October
Habitat: Grassy hills and rocky slopes
Location: Widespread

Cream Cups
Platystemon californicus
Flower size: 1-1 1/2 inches
Plant height: 4-12 inches
Leaf length: 1-3 inches
Season: March - May
Habitat: Meadows and grassy hills
Location: Hikes 24, 25, 26

Other common yellow wildflowers are

False Lupine ..... Mar-May, 2 feet, yellow pea flower, 3 leaflets
Footsteps of Spring ..... Jan-May, 4 inches, low growing, yellow flower
Mariposa Lily ..... May-June, 14 inches, flower with 3 yellow petals
Tree Poppy ..... Feb-June, 3-9 feet shrub, flowers with 4 petals

Gold Fields
Lasthenia californica
Flower size: 1 inch
Plant height: 8 inches
Leaf length: 1/2-1 inch
Season: March - June
Habitat: Meadows and grassy hills
Location: Hikes 13, 14, 20, 26

Monkeyflower or Bush Monkeyflower
Mimulus aurantiacus
Flower size: 1 1/2-2 inches
Plant height: 2-5 feet
Leaf length: 1-3 inches
Season: March - August
Habitat: Chaparral
Location: Widespread

Mule Ears
Wyethia glabra
Flower size: 2 1/2 inches
Plant height: 1-2 feet
Leaf length: 12-20 inches
Season: March - June
Habitat: Woody or brushy areas
Location: Hikes 3, 4, 23, 24, 25, 28

Sun Cups
Camissonia ovata
Flower size: 1/2-1 inch
Plant height: 2-7 inches
Leaf length: 1-4 inches
Season: February - May
Habitat: Grassy hills
Location: Hikes 4, 5, 25, 26, 30

A10 Pink - Red Wildflowers

Checkerbloom
Sidalcea malvaeflora
Flower size: 1 inch
Plant height: 1-2 feet
Leaf length: 1 inch
Season: March - May
Habitat: Open grassy hills
Location: Widespread

Farewell to Spring or Clarkia
Clarkia purpurea ssp. *quadrivulnera*
Flower size: 1-1 1/2 inches
Plant height: 6-15 inches
Leaf length: 1/2-2 inches
Season: May - August
Habitat: Brushy or grassy slopes
Location: Common

Chinese Houses
Collinsia heterophylla
Flower size: 1/2 inch
Plant height: 8-12 inches
Leaf length: 1/2-2 inches
Season: April - May
Habitat: Shaded canyons, wooded
Location: Hikes 12, 22, 23, 25, 26, 28

Other common pink - red wildflowers are

Clintonia ..... Apr-June, 18 inches, shiny leaves, pink flower clusters
Indian Warrior ..... Jan-Apr, 10 inches, fern-like leaves, red flowers
Red Larkspur ..... Mar-June, 18 inches, red 1 inch flower with spur
Wood Rose ..... May-July, 30 inches, shrub with prickles on branches

Columbine
Aquilegia formosa
Flower size: 1 inch
Plant height: 1-2 feet
Leaf length: 2 inches
Season: April - June
Habitat: Brushy slopes, moist woods
Location: Hikes 5, 11, 23, 25

Indian Paintbrush
Castilleja franciscana
Flower size: 1-1 1/2 inches
Plant height: 8-16 inches
Leaf length: 1-3 inches
Season: March - June
Habitat: Brushy or wooded hills
Location: Widespread

Shooting Star
Dodecatheon hendersonii
Flower size: 1 inch
Plant height: 8-16 inches
Leaf length: basal leaves, 2-6 inches
Season: February - April
Habitat: Moist slopes
Location: Common

Trillium
Trilllium chloropetalum
Flower size: 2-4 inches
Plant height: 8-16 inches
Leaf length: 3 leaves, 3-6 inches
Season: February - March
Habitat: Moist wooded slopes
Location: Widespread

A11 Blue - Purple Wildflowers

Blue Dicks
Dichelostemma pulchellum
Flower size: 1 inch
Plant height: 1-2 feet
Leaf length: 6-16 inches
Season: March - June
Habitat: Open or wooded hills
Location: Widespread

Blue-eyed Grass
Sisyrinchium bellum
Flower size: 1/2-1 inch
Plant height: 6-18 inches
Leaf length: 4-24 inches
Season: March - May
Habitat: Open grassy hills
Location: Widespread

Douglas Iris
Iris douglasiana
Flower size: 2-3 inches
Plant height: 6-18 inches
Leaf length: 6-18 inches
Season: March - May
Habitat: Open grassy hills
Location: Widespread, common

Other common blue - purple wildflowers are

Baby Blue-Eyes ..... Mar-May, 8 inches, pale blue 1 inch flowers
Brodiaea ..... Apr-June, 18 inches, spreading cluster of purple flowers
Forget-me-not ..... Feb-June, 12 inches, clusters of small flowers
Slink Pod ..... Jan-Feb, 4 inches, broad spotted leaves, purple flower

Hound's Tongue
Cynoglossum grande
Flower size: 1/2 inch
Plant height: 1-3 feet
Leaf length: 3-6 inches
Season: February - April
Habitat: Moist woods, brushy slopes
Location: Widespread, common

Larkspur
Delphinium hesperium
Flower size: 1 inch with spur
Plant height: 1-2 feet
Leaf length: 1 inch
Season: April - May
Habitat: Clay soil, grassy hills
Location: Hikes 6, 21, 23, 24, 25, 28, 30

Lupine
Lupinus nanus
Flower size: 3-4 inches
Plant height: 4-20 inches
Leaf length: 1/2-1 inch
Season: March - May
Habitat: Grassy hills and fields
Location: Widespread

Mission Bells
Fritillaria lanceolata
Flower size: 1-1 1/2 inches
Plant height: 1-2 feet
Leaf length: leaves in whorls, 2-6 inches
Season: January - March
Habitat: Shaded woody or brushy slopes
Location: Hikes 6, 14, 15, 19, 20, 28, 32

A12 Chaparral Community

The chaparral community, comprised mostly of chamise, manzanita, ceanothus and oaks, makes up about 25% of the native cover on Mt Tamalpais. The three major conditions favoring chaparral growth over other plant groups are summer drought, thin soil and periodic fires. Chaparral are excellent drought resistant plants that often have small

evergreen leaves with a waxy, shiny or hairy covering to prevent water loss and long roots to tap moisture from surrounding areas.

Chamise
Chamise, *Adenostoma fasciculatum*, the most common shrub of the chaparral community, is 3-10 feet tall with tiny, needle-like leaves, and small white flowers that start blooming in May.

Manzanita
Arctostaphylos spp., five species of manzanita found on Mt Tamalpais are all members of the chaparral community. Manzanita shrubs are 3-10 feet tall with simple, oval-shaped leaves and small solitary urn-shaped flowers that start blooming in December. The trunks of manzanita shrubs are very distinctive with a smooth, deep reddish-brown bark.

Ceanothus
Ceanothus spp., six species of ceanothus, or California lilac, are found on Mt Tamalpais and these shrubs range in size from 1-15 feet. They have shiny leaves, often with 3 veins diverging from the base. The fragrant flower clusters vary from white to blue to purple and start showing up in February.

Oaks
There are several species of oaks (and some hybrid species) on Mt Tamalpais and four of these are found in the chaparral community. Surprisingly, one of the oaks found in chaparral, the canyon live oak is the same species that becomes a majestic 50 foot hilltop oak under

better conditions. Three other oaks found in this community are the leather oak, chaparral oak and scrub oak. The leather oak, *Quercus durata*, is restricted to serpentine areas.

Other common chaparral plants include toyon, bush monkeyflower, yerba santa, chaparral pea, huckleberry, tree poppy, pitcher sage and Indian paintbrush.

Although the chaparral communities of Mt Tamalpais are healthy, they are decreasing in size, especially at lower elevations. Because there has not been a large fire on the mountain in a long time, oak-bay hardwoods and Douglas fir trees have invaded many chaparral areas where soil and moisture conditions are adequate. This process can be seen on several trails including the TCC Trail, Hike 8, Redwood Trail, Hike 3, and the International Trail, Hike 15. However, deer are chaparral's friend. Deer like to eat hardwood acorns and first-year hardwood and Douglas fir growth.

The largest chaparral stands are located high on the south-facing slopes of Mt Tamalpais and can be seen on the Matt Davis Trail, Hike 7, Rock Spring Trail, Hike 9 and 15, and East Peak Loop, Hike 16. Serpentine versions of the chaparral community can be seen on the Simmons Trail, Hike 13 and Benstein Trail, Hike 15.

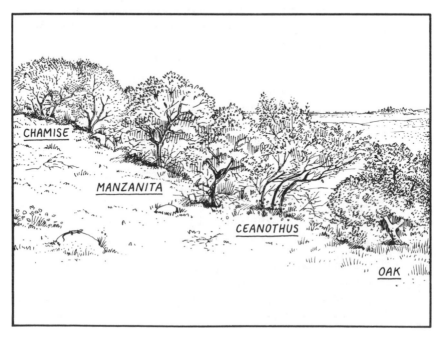

A13 Oak - Bay Hardwood Community

The oak - bay hardwood community, composed primarily of oaks and bay, with some madrone and tanoak (related to true oaks), makes up about 25% of Mt Tamalpais flora. This vegetation type is also referred to as the broadleaf evergreen community in contrast with the needled conifer community of redwood and Douglas fir. However, the hardwood and conifer communities are often found mixed together and this mixture is very common, representing 40% of the vegetation on Mt Tamalpais.

The conditions favoring both the oak - bay hardwood and the mixed hardwood - conifer forest are good winter rainfall and deep soil, required for developing extensive root systems.

Oak

Several oaks grow on Mt Tamalpais with the coast live oak, *Quercus agrifolia*, the most common. It is a large 30-75 foot tree with a broad round crown and 1-2 inch oval-cupped leaves. The acorns are slender and pointed, and mature in one season.

Other oaks found here include the evergreen canyon live oak (or goldcup oak), chaparral oak and the deciduous California black oak.

Bay

California bay or laurel, *Umbellularia californica*, is companion to the oaks. Its dark green, lance shaped leaves have a distinctive odor when crushed and can be used to flavor beans and stews. The tree is adaptable to most light conditions and is increasing in number, usually at the expense of oaks.

Two deciduous residents of this community are the big leaf maple and buckeye. Two common evergreen members of this community are the madrone, with its distinctive smooth red bark and shiny leaves, and the tanoak.

Many shrubs, herbs and grasses are found in the understory of the hardwood forest as these trees do not form the dense canopy of the redwood - Douglas fir community. Some common shrubs are coffeeberry, California hazel, ocean spray, poison oak and wood rose.

The diversity of plant life leads to a diversity of mammals and birds. Seeing mule deer, squirrels and jack rabbits is an ordinary occurrence, bobcats and grey fox an extraordinary one.

Under certain conditions, just as the hardwoods invade chaparral, the hardwoods themselves can be replaced by Douglas fir. Douglas fir is a natural successor to hardwoods because it grows taller and can shade them out. Bays can be an exception. If bay trees are well established, they form a dense enough crown to restrict Douglas fir seedlings and will repel an invasion.

Several interrelated factors determine the survival and success of communities; seed production, soil and moisture conditions, light, wind, fires, deer, rodents, insects and birds. For example, oak seeds or acorns, are highly nutritious and have long been a food source for man, deer, rodents and birds. Overpopulation of one or more acorn-eaters can severely limit oak reproduction. In the struggle for success in the hardwood community, bay, tanoak and madrone appear to be increasing, while oaks are decreasing in number.

There are several excellent examples of oak - bay hardwood forest around the lakes, Hikes 18, 26 and 28, along Deer Park Rd, Hikes 23 and 24, on the Old Mine Trail, Hike 10 and around Rock Spring, Hikes 13 and 14.

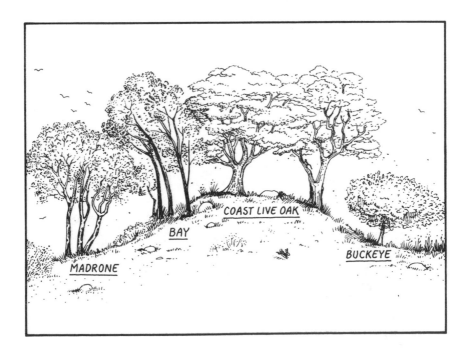

A14 Redwood - Douglas Fir Conifer Community

The redwood - Douglas fir conifer community makes up only about 5% of the vegetation on Mt Tamalpais. However, there are many more areas where redwoods and especially Douglas fir have invaded other communities, usually forming a mixed hardwood - conifer community. Year-round water is the limiting factor in the distribution of these conifers. Winter rains and summer creeks or summer fog are necessary for redwood growth and to a lesser extent, growth of Douglas fir. Summer fog is like summer rain as the fog condenses on the needles high in the crown canopy, then drips to the ground providing up to 20 inches of water per year.

Redwood

The coastal redwood, *Sequoia sempervirens*, is the world's tallest tree reaching over 350 feet, although the tallest redwood in Muir Woods stands but 258 feet. Branches of redwoods form flat sprays with dark, shiny green, one inch pointed needles. The cones are small, from 1-2 inches long. Redwoods have a shallow root system spreading out from the base and severe winters will leave a few trees toppled. Redwoods are fire resistant because of their thick non-resinous bark, moist wood core and because of branch height.

The phenols in the bark and wood act as a natural insecticide that discourages insects and consequently limits surrounding bird life. Not only do redwoods form a dense canopy that shades and restricts growth on the forest floor, but also the decomposition of its needles produces a rich humus that favors acid-loving plants like redwood sorrel, trillium, clintonia and several species of ferns.

Douglas Fir

Douglas fir, *Pseudotsuga menziesii*, is a conifer and not a true fir tree. Usually, wherever you find redwoods, you will find Douglas fir, only in less moist conditions. Douglas fir grows to heights of 250 feet with a pyramid shaped crown. The one inch needles grow out at any angle and the 2-3 inch cones have a mouse-like tail that helps to distinguish them from redwoods.

95

Because of hardwood invasion, Douglas fir forests on Mt Tamalpais live in a delicate balance of nature. Parent seed trees start the survival process by scattering seed for the next generation of trees. However, if hardwoods, especially bay trees have invaded the understory, then the Douglas fir seedlings will not get enough light to survive. Deer help keep the hardwoods in check by nibbling acorns and young sprouts. Fire forms an alternative control of hardwood growth. However, the fire conditions must be just right and often enough to restrict hardwood growth without removing the Douglas fir seed trees.

Tanoak and big leaf maple are two other trees found searching for light in the conifer forest. In a deeply shaded forest, tanoaks take on the appearance of small shrubs, while under ideal conditions, they can become100 foot trees.

The redwood - Douglas fir conifer community can be found in three major areas on Mt Tamalpais; Muir Woods, Hikes 1, 2, 3 and 4, Steep Ravine, Hike 11 and in the Alpine Lake - Cataract Creek area, Hikes 27 and 32.

A15 A Quick Guide To Flora

Index of Wildflowers

Baby Blue-eyes ... Mar-May, 8", pale blue 1 inch flowers
Blue Dicks ... Mar-June, 18", blue 1 inch cluster of flowers
Blue-eyed Grass ... Mar-May, 12", blue flower , yellow center
Brodiaea ... Apr-June, 18", spreading cluster of purple flowers
Buttercup ... Feb-May, 12", flower with shiny yellow petals
Bush Monkeyflower ... Mar-Aug, 3', yellow flower, sticky leaves
Calochortus ... Mar-May, 6", white to lavender flower, basal leaf
Checkerbloom ... Mar-May, 12", pink 1" flower, lobed leaves
Cream Cups ... Mar-May, 8", creamy yellow 1 inch flowers
Crimson Clover ... Apr-June, 12", bright red 1" flower, non-native
Chinese Houses ... Apr-May, 10", pink and white flowers in tiers
Clarkia ... May-Aug, 10", bright pink flower, blooms late
Clintonia ... Apr-June, 18", shiny leaves, pink flower clusters
Columbine ... Apr-June, 18", flowers nodding, red and yellow
Douglas Iris ... Mar-May, 12", purple 2 inch flower
Fairy Bells ... Feb-July, 2', greenish white, bell-shaped flowers
False Lupine ... Mar-May, 2', yellow pea flower, 3 leaflets
Fiddleneck ... Mar-June, 12", orange flowers coiled at end of stem
Filaree ... Mar-Aug, 4", pink-lavender flower, grassy hillsides
Footsteps of Spring ... Jan-May, 4", low growing, yellow flower
Forget-me-not ... Feb-June, 12", light blue flowers, non-native
Gold Fields ... Mar-June, 8", small yellow daisy-like flower
Hound's Tongue ... Feb-Apr, 2', large leaves, blue flowers
Indian Paintbrush ... Mar-June, 12", red orange flower
Indian Warrior ... Jan-Apr, 10", fern-like leaves, red flowers
Larkspur ... Apr-May, 18", blue 1 inch flower with spur
Lupine ... Mar-May, 12", divided leaves, blue pea flower
Mariposa Lily .. May-June, 14", flower with 3 yellow petals
Milkmaids ... Jan-Mar, 16", most common white flower plant
Mission Bells ... Jan-Mar, 18", purple bell-shaped flower
Modesty ... Mar-May, 8", trailing plant, 1/8 inch white flowers
Morning Glory ... Mar-Sept, 2', twining vine, pinkish white flowers
Mule Ears ... Mar-June, 18", large leaves, yellow sunflower
Popcorn Flower ... Apr-May, 12", small white flowers
Poppy, California ... Mar-Oct, 12", yellow cup-shaped flower
Red Larkspur ... Mar-June, 18", red 1 inch flower with spur
Redwood Sorrel ... Mar-June, 6", pink flowers, clover-like leaves
Sanicle ... Mar-June, 12", yellow or purple flower balls, lobed leaves
Shooting Star ... Feb-Apr, 12", pink petals turned back
Slim Solomon ... Feb-Apr, 12", bright green leaves, white flower
Slink Pod ... Jan-Feb, 4", broad spotted leaves, purple flower
Star Flower ... Mar-July, 8", whorl of leaves, pink flowers
White Wild Onion ... Apr-May, 8", white flower, onion odor, non-native

Sun Cups ... Feb-May, 5", basal leaves, yellow cupped flower
Trillium ... Feb-Mar, 12", leaves and flowers in sets of three
Woodland Star ... Mar-May, 16", small white star-like flower
Yarrow ... Apr-Sept, 18", fern-like leaves, white flower cluster
Zigadene ... Feb-Apr, 16", robust plant with white flowers

Index of Shrubs and Trees
Bay ... Tree to 100' tall, dark green aromatic leaves
Big Leaf Maple ... Deciduous tree 15-90' tall, deeply lobed leaves
Black Oak, California ... Deciduous tree 30-75' , deeply lobed leaves
Broom ... Non-native invasive shrub to 9', yellow pea flowers in spring
Buckeye ... Deciduous tree or shrub, fragrant flowers in May and June
Canyon Live Oak ... (or Goldcup Oak) to 60', leaves grey to gold beneath
Ceanothus ... Shrub to 15', spring flowers in clusters
Chamise ... Shrub 3-10' high, needle-like leaves
Chaparral Oak ... Shrub 3-10', oval leaf, edge smooth or serrated
Chaparral Pea ... Spiny shrub 2-6', bright pink pea flowers
Chinquapin ... Shrub or tree 6-60' tall, leaves green above, gold below
Coast Live Oak ... Tree 30-75', oval cupped-shaped leaves
Coffeeberry ... Rounded shrub 3-12' tall, ripe berries black or red
Coulter Pine ... Tree 50-75', large cones, needles in bunches of 3
Coyote Brush ... Shrub of coastal scrub 3-12' high, toothed leaves
Douglas Fir ... Tree to 250' tall, flat 1" needles, 2-3" cones
Elk Clover ... Deciduous shrub to 4', very large leaves, moist areas
Hazel,California ... Deciduous shrub 6-18' , leaves softly hairy
Huckleberry ... Shrub 3-8' tall, oval shiny leaves, edible fruit in fall
Leather Oak ... Shrub 3-9', small oval leaves with spiny teeth
Manzanita ... Shrub with reddish brown bark, urn-shaped white flower
Madrone ... Tree 15-120' tall, smooth red bark, shiny leaves
Nutmeg, California ... Tree 15-90' tall, stiff pointed needles, fruit 2"
Ocean Spray ... Shrub 4-18' tall, oval leaves toothed, white flower
Pitcher Sage ... Shrub 3' high, bell-shaped white flower
Poison Oak ... Shrub to 9', 3 leaflets, small white flower clusters, climbing
Red Alder ... Deciduous tree 45-75' along stream banks, oval leaf
Redwood ... Tree to 260', branches forming flat sprays, 1" cones
Sargent Cypress ... Tree of serpentine 10-45' , leaves scale-like
Scrub Oak ... Shrub 3-9', oval leaves, shiny above, pale beneath, rare
Silk Tassel Bush ... Shrub to 20', oval leaves, wavy edge, long catkins
Tanoak ... Tree 10-120' with conical crown, veined leaves
Tree Poppy ... Shrub 3-9', leaves gray green, 4 yellow petals in spring
Toyon ... Shrub 6-30' high, toothed leaves, red summer berries
Wood Rose ... Shrub 3' high with prickles, small 1" pink flowers
Western Azalea ... Deciduous shrub to 9', fragrant flowers in June
Yerba Santa ... Aromatic shrub 3' tall, dark green leaves, white flower

All trees and shrubs are evergreen unless described as deciduous.

A16 Bibliography

Aker, R. Sir Francis Drake at Drakes Bay. Drakes Navigator Guild, 1978.

Bakker, E.S. An Island Called California. University of California Press, 1971.

Bowen, O.E. Jr. Rocks and Minerals of the San Francisco Bay Region. University of California Press, 1966.

Brockman, C. F. Trees of North America. Golden Press, 1968.

Gilliam, H. Weather of the San Francisco Bay Region. University of California Press, 1962.

Gudde, E.G. California Place Names. University of California Press, 1969.

Howell, J.T. Marin Flora. University of California Press, 1970.

Kruckeberg, A.R. California Serpentines. University of California Press. 1984.

Mason, J. The Making of Marin. North Shore Books, 1975.

McHoul, L. Wildflowers Of Marin. The Tamal Land Press, 1979.

Morrato, M.J. California Archaeology. Academic Press, 1984.

Munz, P.A. A California Flora. University of California Press, 1959.

Niehaus, T.F. & Ripper, C.L. A Field Guide to Pacific Wildflowers. Houghton Mifflin, 1976.

Olson, R. The History of Mount Tamalpais. A thesis presented to the faculty of the Consortium of the California State University, 1985.

Teather, L. Place Names of Marin. Scottwall Associates, 1986.

Whitnah, D.L. An Outdoor Guide to the San Francisco Bay Area. Wilderness Press, 1976.

... Handbook of North American Indians. Vol. 8, Smithsonian Institute, 1978.

... Environmental Planning Study. Marin Muncipal Water District, 1976.

About the authors

Kay Martin has a degree in botany from San Francisco State University and works as a volunteer docent for Bay Shore Studies. She is active with the California Native Plant Society and is a member of the Tamalpa Runners. In training for three marathons, she has logged several thousand miles running the trails of Mt Tamalpais.

Don Martin teaches physics, astronomy, energy science and computer science at Marin Community College. He is director of the Science Computer Center and has co-authored four computer books, all published by Howard W. Sams.

The Martins are members of the Sierra Club, Audubon Society and the Mt Tamalpais History Project. They have four grown children.

Bob Johnson is a well-known Marin County cartoonist and illustrator. He draws cartoons for several newspapers and was creator of the cartoon strip, "Hello Carol." He has illustrated over thirty plant books, twenty computer books and a variety of other books, posters and artwork.

ORDER FORM

Martin Press
PO Box 2109
San Anselmo, CA 94960

Here is the price schedule for ordering additional copies
of this book.

    1 - 2 copies at $8.95 each.

    3 - 5 copies at $7.95 each.

    6 - 10 copies at $6.95 each.

    11 or more copies at $6.45 each.

Price includes shipping at book rate. California residents
please add 6% sales tax.

Number of books ordered: _____

Amount Enclosed: _____ (Check or money order)

Name:_____

Address:_____

_____ZIP:_____

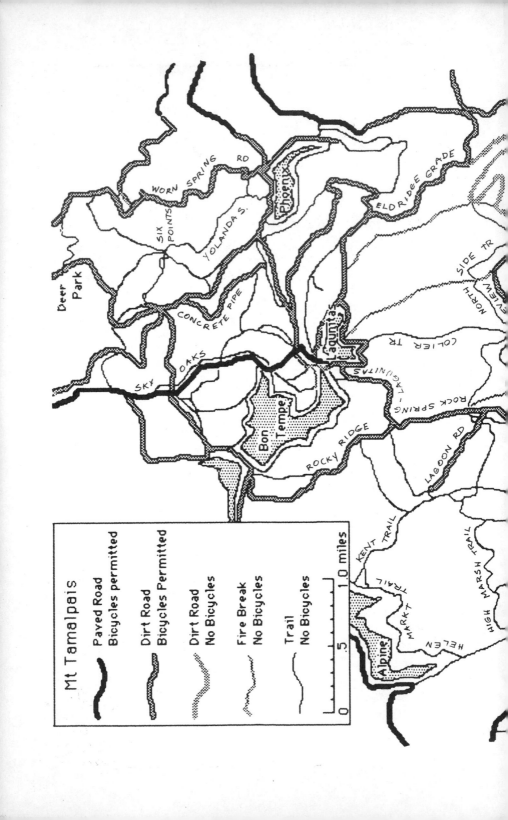